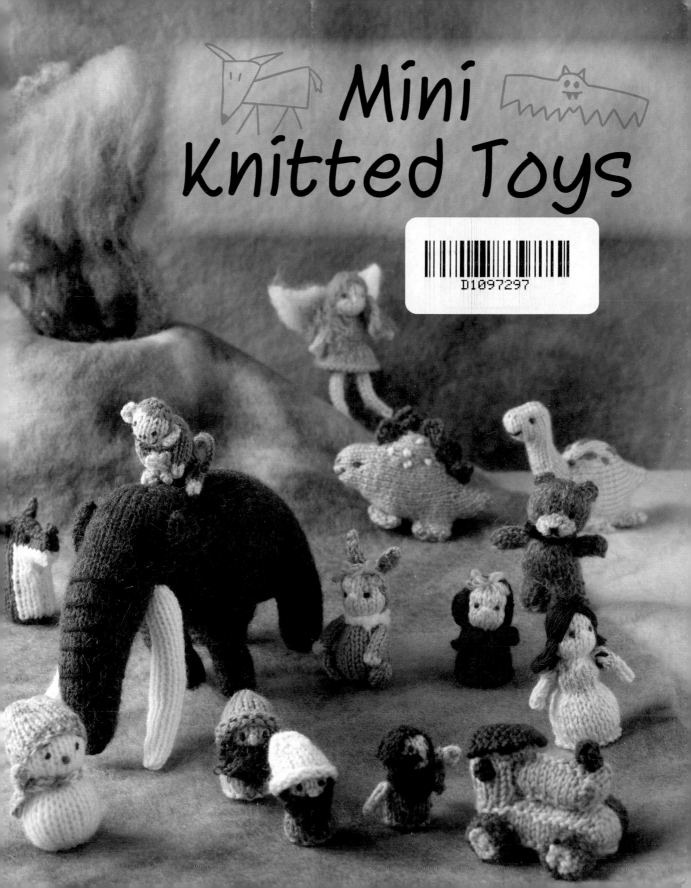

Mini Knitted Toys

Dedication

I would like to dedicate this book to my sons, who have given me lots of inspiration, encouragement and their honest opinions.

Sachiyo Ishii

Mini Knitted Toys

Over 30 cute and easy knitting patterns

Search Press

First published in 2016

Search Press Limited
Wellwood, North Farm Road,
Tunbridge Wells, Kent TN2 3DR

Print ISBN: 978-1-78221-145-7
eBook ISBN: 978-1-78126-419-5

Suppliers
If you have difficulty in obtaining any of the materials or equipment mentioned in this book, then please visit the Search Press website for details of suppliers:
www.searchpress.com

You are invited to view the author's work at:
etsy.com/shop/sachiyoishii
visit her website at: knitsbysachi.com
visit her blog at: knitsbysachi.wordpress.com
search for KnitsbySachi on www.ravelry.com
or search for Knits by Sachi on Facebook

Printed in China

Acknowledgements

I would like to thank everyone in the Search Press team, especially Katie French and Becky Shackleton, for helping me to create such a wonderful book. I would also like to thank the designer, Juan Hayward, and the photographer, Paul Bricknell, for the beautiful layout and photography. Thanks also go to Jacky Edwards for her pattern checking. Lastly, I would like to thank Carole Weighill, of Threadneedles in East Grinstead, who kindly lent us some of the toys from her shop to use as props.

Contents

Teddy buddies

Cosy snowmen

Awesome aeroplanes

Colourful chameleons

Little Red Riding Hood and the wolf

Three little pigs

Snuggly pandas

Bouncing balls

Scrumptious cupcakes

Choo-choo train

Cute cats and marvellous mice

Balancing baby clowns

Doggy buddies

Cheeky monkeys

Yellow submarine

Nuts about squirrels

Beach bunnies

Fun finger puppets

Deadly dinosaurs

Perfect penguins

Alien invasion!

Mousey mates

Pretty parrot

Dressing-up time!

Cuddly kangaroos

Playful puppies

Curious cats

Fabulous fairies

Up-and-away!

Prehistoric playtime

Castle under siege!

Snow White and the seven dwarves

Introduction

I started this book by creating small toys that are simple to make and a good size for little hands. It's always nice to find a way to use your stash and what's more, with these patterns you can make something cute in just a few hours. But as I proceeded I decided that I also wanted to include projects of different sizes and styles. I would like many people to enjoy this book and so I tried to create something for everyone: at the beginning of the book there are very simple knits that use very basic knitting techniques, we then move on to patterns that are a little more involved and then, towards the end of the book, there are much larger projects with different components and characters.

You may want to make these toys for a child or as a gift for a friend. I design toys mainly to please myself as my boys are too grown up to play with them now, although I do know that they are tickled by some of my more quirky designs! Knitting toys is fantastic because you get to have lots of fun during the creation process and you also get to make someone happy when you present them with your unique handmade gift. This is what I am aiming for with this book – to make you knitters happy.

You can be fairly relaxed with knitting the pieces here. You do not need to follow each pattern diligently: if you miss a stitch in one row, you can add a stitch in the next. If you decide you want to improvise the pattern, feel free! Use the colour of your choice and go wild with your imagination.

In order to make up the toys you will need to assemble them, sew them and embroider them. You may find these processes a little fiddly at first, but please don't be put off – I can assure you that the end result will be worth it. And one final thing – please bear in mind that some of the toys may be too small to give to a very young child – always refer to the finished size and cautions written on the page before you start to knit.

I do hope you enjoy this book.
Happy knitting!

Materials and tools

Yarn

All the toys in this book are knitted with DK (8-ply) yarn, and you don't need much to create each toy; some require less than 5g ($^1/_6$oz), which is equivalent to a skein of tapestry wool. The largest project is the castle (see pages 100–107) and it requires about 60g (2oz). You may already have oddments of yarn left over from previous projects and these toys are the perfect way to use up your stash. I prefer knitting with DK (8-ply) yarn, which is why I've used it throughout the book, but you can use any weight of yarn you like – simply adjust the needle size accordingly.

I have mainly used 100 per cent wool yarns in the projects, as I love the feel of wool and the colour tones it can create. If you are making toys for children you might wish to choose natural materials. I also find wool is the easiest when you want to make stitches neat and even. Feel free to experiment with alpaca, mohair, cotton or synthetic yarns for different texture. I have also used chunky fleecy yarn for some projects. This can be replaced with mohair or bouclé yarn if you prefer. If you only need a small amount of certain colours, tapestry yarn may be a good choice.

Stuffing

I mostly use washed wool fleece to stuff my knitted toys. It's ideal as it is natural, has plenty of bounce, fills any shapes well and is inexpensive. If you cannot get hold of wool fleece, you can use polyester toy filling of course, which is readily available from craft shops.

Needles

A pair of double-pointed needles size 2.75mm (UK 12, US 2)

This is the needle size I used for all the toys in the book. Your knitting tension (gauge) needs to be fairly tight, so that when the toys are sewn up the stuffing is not visible through the stitches. If you struggle with knitting DK (8-ply) yarn on fine needles, experiment with a larger size. Some knitters naturally knit tighter than others and the tension (gauge) will also differ depending on the yarn you use. I have given a general tension (gauge) as a guide on page 14, but I haven't specified tensions (gauges) for any of the projects in this book, as the size of the finished projects doesn't really matter.

Crochet hook, size 3.0mm (UK 11, US C/2 or D/3) or similar

Some of the projects require you to use a crochet hook for a few simple processes: making chains and picking up stitches from a knitted piece. You don't need to know how to create any crochet stitches for this book.

Sharp needle

I recommend that you use a chenille or tapestry needle with a sharp point, as it will be easier to work through your tightly knitted toys than a blunt-ended needle. You can also use the same needle for embroidering. Your toys will be sewn up using the same yarn that you knitted them with, ideally using yarn ends, if you have left them. It is a good idea to make a habit of leaving fairly long ends when you cast on and fasten off.

Other tools

Wooden chopstick

A simple but incredibly effective tool, a chopstick is by far the best instrument for pushing stuffing into your toys, as you can use it to reach into slender body parts. If you don't have one, you could use a large knitting needle or a pencil.

Scissors

Essential for trimming yarn ends when sewing up.

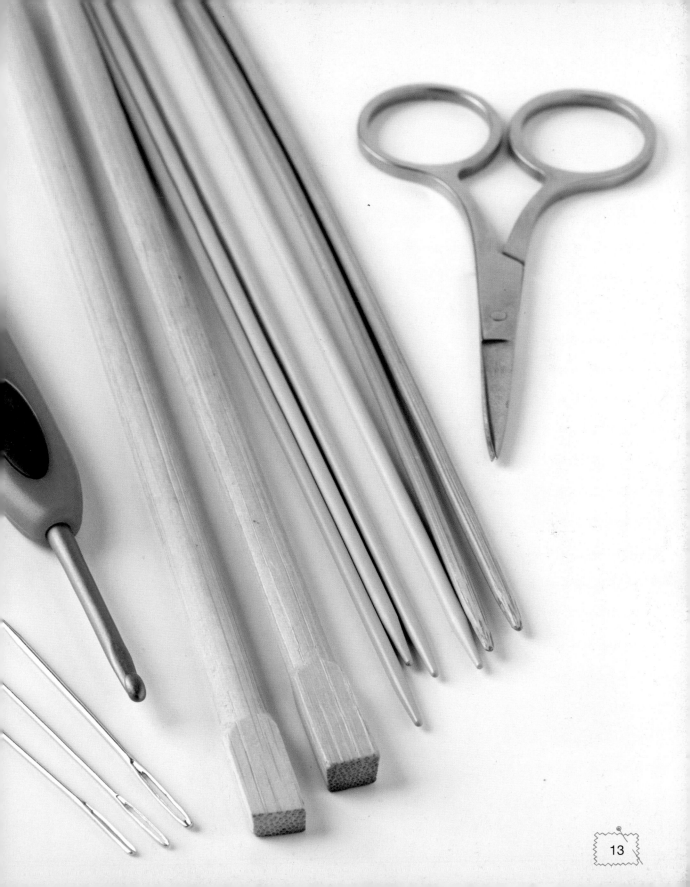

Basic knitting

The stitches used in this book are just very basic knit and purl. It still amazes me that it is possible to turn small amounts of yarn into something really special using just these two simple techniques. All the toys are knitted flat with two double-pointed knitting needles.

Increasing and decreasing

To increase one stitch, knit or purl into the front loop and the back loop of the same stitch. This will not create a hole, unlike picking up between the stitches or bringing the yarn forward. To decrease one stitch, knit or purl two stitches together.

Yarn ends

Always leave long ends when casting on and fastening off, for sewing up the piece later. Tuck any unsewn yarn ends inside the body of the toy before you sew it up; not only can you reduce waste in this way, but the colour will match and so the stuffing will be less visible.

Tension (gauge)

This is only a rough guide and it is not essential to follow it, as long as you keep your own tension consistent throughout. I work to a tension of 12 sts and 16 rows over a 4cm (1½in) square, in st/st, using 2.75mm (UK 12, US 2) knitting needles.

Basic crochet

I have used only a couple of simple crochet techniques throughout: making chains and slip stitch.

Tip

Stretch or rest your hands from time to time if you are not used to knitting tight pieces with small needles. Open and close your hands to exercise them and to prevent them becoming stiff or sore.

Abbreviations

Knitting

st/st	stocking stitch (knit on right-side rows, purl on wrong-side rows)
k	knit
p	purl
inc	increase
dec	decrease
k2tog	knit 2 stitches together
p2tog	purl 2 stitches together
kf/b	knit into front and back of stitch (increasing one stitch)
st(s)	stitch(es)
g-st	garter stitch (knit every row)
pf/b	purl into front and back of stitch (increasing one stitch)
skpo	slip 1 stitch, knit 1 stitch, pass the slipped stitch over (decreasing one stitch)
yf	yarn forward
yb	yarn back
sl1	slip 1 stitch
RS	right side
WS	wrong side
kf/b/f	knit into front and back and front of stitch (increasing two stitches)

Crochet

ch	chain
ss	slip stitch: insert hook into chain and wrap yarn round hook. Draw a new loop through both the chain and the loop on the hook, ending with one loop on the hook

Sewing up and stuffing

Not all of the human figures in the book are the same size. Snow White is 8cm (3¼in) tall (see page 108), while others, such as the cavemen, are only 4cm (1½in) tall (see page 96). However, the basic method for making all the figures is the same: you will sew and shape the body, stuff, flatten the base and create facial features in the same way. Make sure you read through these instructions before you start, so that you are familiar with the process. I have used an overcast stitch throughout.

Creating the head, body and skirt

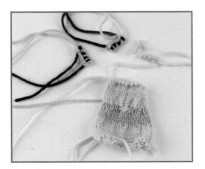

Here are the head, body, arms and sleeves needed for Snow White (see page 108).

1 Using the skin colour fasten-off yarn end, start at the top of the head and start to sew the seam using overcast stitch.

2 Stop when you reach the end of the skin colour head section.

3 Use the blue fasten-off yarn end to continue to sew the seam down the back of the body. Finish stitching when you reach the end of the blue section.

4 Starting now at the base of the piece, use the yellow cast-on yarn end to work a gathering thread along the bottom.

5 Pull the thread tight to draw in your stitches.

6 Complete the base by sewing outwards from the centre of the circle to the edge, joining the two open edges, as shown.

7 Roll a small ball of stuffing and push it into the head, using a chopstick or needle. This will help you to avoid creating a thick neck.

8 Continue to stuff the body, a small amount at a time, until it feels firm. Leave out one yarn end of each colour, and tuck all the others inside. Sew the rest of the back seam.

9 Work a gathering stitch all the way around the neck, at the row indicated in the pattern.

10 Pull the yarn tight to draw in the neck. Take the yarn up to the eye line.

11 Work a gathering stitch along the eyeline. Pull the yarn tight to create the shape of the face.

13 Take the yellow yarn end, and pass it through the body and out through the centre of the base. Then, take it back through the base and bring it out at Snow White's back.

12 Take the yarn to nose height, and backstitch three times on the same spot to create a nose.

14 Pull the yarn firmly to dent the base of the body. This will help Snow White to stand upright.

15 To complete the base, take the yarn back out through the centre again and cut the end.

16 To create Snow White's waist, run a gathering stitch around the lowest line of blue stitches, and pull firmly to draw it in. Fasten off the yarn end.

Creating the sleeves and arms

1 Weave the red yarn ends into the piece to secure them, then trim them off.

2 Wrap a sleeve piece around one of the arms, and using the blue cast-on end, secure in place with a couple of stitches.

3 Use the blue cast-on yarn end to sew the underarm seam of the sleeve. Hide the skin colour yarn inside the arm, and the fasten-off end of the blue yarn inside the sleeve; trim the ends. Leave the remaining blue yarn end for now.

4 Repeat for the other arm. Using the remaining blue yarn end, sew each arm in place, with the seam facing down. Fasten off.

Creating the hair, eyes and bow

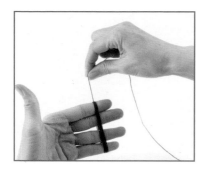

1 Wrap a length of fine brown fingering (2-ply) yarn around your fingers, twenty-five to thirty times to create a loop.

2 Position this centrally on top of Snow White's head, to ensure that you are happy with the length.

3 Using a length of matching yarn, sew the hair in place along a central parting using backstitch.

4 Secure the hair at the sides of the head with a few stitches, to create the style. Secure the yarn and trim the ends.

5 Use dark brown DK (8-ply) yarn to make a French knot for each eye, taking the needle point out through a strand of yarn on the face, not between the stitches; after creating the first eye, take the yarn through the head to create the second, then take it out of the back of the head to fasten off.

6 Take a length of red yarn through Snow White's head, and sew a long stitch over the top to create a hair band. Bring the yarn out at the top centre of her head.

7 Take the yarn over the hair band and through the head, creating a loop – do not pull this tight. Instead, leaving it loose, backstitch at the base to secure it. Repeat a second time to create the second loop of the bow. Secure the yarn and fasten off.

Key techniques

Creating knitted eyes

Most of the characters' eyes are simply French knots, but some, such as those for the panda, are made in the following way:

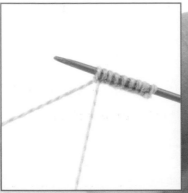

1 Cast on the number of stitches given in your pattern. Thread the yarn end on to a sewing needle.

2 Transfer your stitches on to the sewing needle: pass the sewing needle right the way through all your stitches.

3 Push the sewing needle in through the same end of the stitches and take it out from the outer edge. Pull tight to connect the ends.

4 You should now have created a half-circle shape. Put the sewing needle through the centre of the shape and bring it out at the outer edge.

5 Repeat step 4 to create a circle.

Creating an i-cord

I-cords are used for many things within the book, from the tail of a mouse to Snow White's arms, so this is a great skill to learn.

1 Cast on the required number of stitches according to your pattern, using double-pointed needles.

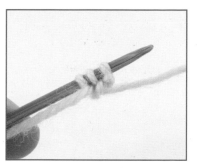

2 Do not turn the needle, instead, slide the stitches to the other end. Bring the working yarn behind the stitches.

3 Knit one row of stitches.

4 Continue to knit the stitches until the i-cord reaches the correct length for your pattern.

5 Carefully transfer your stitches on to a sewing needle.

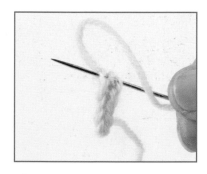

6 Take the needle through the last row of stitches a second time.

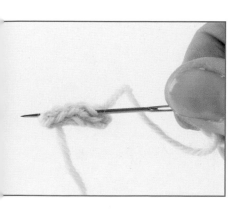

7 Finish by weaving the yarn tails inside the i-cord, and trim the ends.

Basic embroidery

Some simple embroidery stitches are used to complete the toys. I most commonly use fingering (4-ply) yarn or DK (8-ply) yarn to embroider faces.

French knots

These are used for most of the toys' eyes. Take the needle through the yarn, separating the fibres, instead of taking the needle out between the stitches. This prevents the eye from sinking into the face.

For the human figures, and for toys where I want the eyes to stand out, I have used a full strand of DK (8-ply) yarn, not just two strands.

1 Bring the thread through where the knot is required, at A. Holding the thread between your thumb and finger, wrap it around the needle twice.

2 Hold the thread firmly with your thumb and turn the needle back to A. Insert it as close to A as possible, at B, and pull the thread through to form a knot.

3 Make a small stitch on the wrong side of the fabric before fastening off.

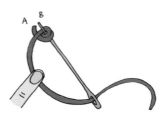

Backstitch

This simple stitch is used to create mouth and nose markings on many of the toys, and colourful back markings on a few others, such as the chameleon (pages 32–33).

1 Bring the needle up at A and pull the thread through. Insert the needle at B and bring it through at C. Pull the thread through the fabric.

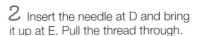

2 Insert the needle at D and bring it up at E. Pull the thread through.

3 Insert the needle at F and bring it up at G. Continue working along the stitch line until it is completed. To finish off, thread your needle through the stitches on the wrong side of your work.

Chain stitch

This is used to create the pattern on the basketball (see page 40).

1 Bring the needle up through the fabric at A and pull the thread through. Insert the needle at B, as close as possible to A, and bring it up at C. Keep the thread under the needle. Pull the thread through gently to form the first chain.

2 Insert the needle at D, as close as possible to C, and bring the needle up at E. Keeping the thread under the needle, pull the thread through gently to form the second chain.

3 Continue in this way, making evenly sized chain stitches, until the line of stitching is complete.

Have fun!

Be innovative and have fun with your mini knitted toys. Mix and match items from the projects: after all, why shouldn't an alien drive a train? Or a panda be friends with a snowman? Don't be afraid to try out your own ideas and improvise with colours, yarns and textures.

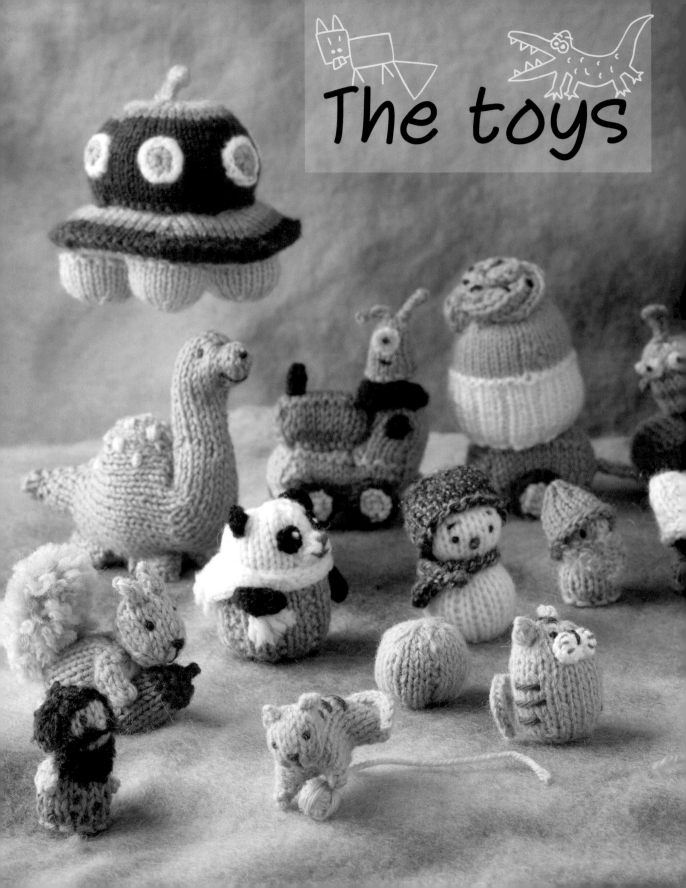

The toys

Teddy buddies

Instructions

The legs, body and head for both bears are all knitted in one piece.

Small teddy

Right leg

Cast on 10 sts with brown and light brown mix yarn and st/st 6 rows, starting with a k row. Break yarn, keep stitches on a spare needle or a stitch holder.

Left leg

Follow the instructions given for the right leg, but do not break off the yarn. With right side facing, place the right leg on the left side of the left leg on the same needle and continue.

Row 7: k5, yf, sl1, yb, turn, sl1, p to end.

Row 8: k across all sts to connect the two legs (20).

Row 9: p5, yb, sl1, yf, turn, sl1, k to end.

Row 10: p (20).

Row 11: k14, yf, sl1, yb, turn, sl1, p8, yb, sl1, yf, turn, sl1, k to end.

Rows 12–15: st/st.

Row 16: (p2tog) to end (10).

Row 17: k.

Row 18: pf/b in each st (20).

Rows 19–26: st/st.

Row 27: (k2tog) to end (10).

Break yarn, draw through sts, pull tightly and fasten off.

Arms: make two

Cast on 6 sts with brown and light brown mix yarn and st/st 6 rows, starting with a k row. Break yarn, draw through sts, pull tightly and fasten off.

Ears: make two

Cast on 8 sts with brown and light brown mix yarn. Break yarn, draw through sts, pull tightly and fasten off.

Muzzle

Cast on 12 sts with beige yarn. Break yarn, draw through sts, pull tightly and fasten off.

Scarf

Cast on 3 sts with dark red yarn and work an i-cord (see page 21) for 10cm (4in).

Break yarn, draw through sts, pull tightly and fasten off.

To make up

Sew the head and body seam, leaving a gap for stuffing. Stuff, avoiding the neck area and close the seam. Work a gathering thread around the neck, pull tightly and fasten off. Sew each leg seam, leaving the cast-on edges unsewn for stuffing. Stuff and close the seam. Attach the muzzle and ears. Using black DK (8-ply) yarn, embroider each eye with a French knot. Take two strands from the black DK (8-ply) yarn and embroider the nose and mouth with short backstitches. Sew in the ends of the scarf neatly and tie the scarf around the neck.

Materials

Small teddy:

DK (8-ply) yarn: 7g (¼oz), brown and light brown mix

Note: For both bears I have used a brown and light brown tweed yarn. Use any colour yarn in your stash.

DK (8-ply) yarn: small amounts of beige, dark red and black

Stuffing

Big teddy:

DK (8-ply) yarn: 10g (⅓oz), brown and light brown mix

DK (8-ply) yarn: small amounts of beige, dark red and black

Stuffing

Size

Small teddy: 7.5cm (3in) tall

Big teddy: 9cm (3½in) tall

Additional equipment

A spare needle or stitch holder

Difficulty level

Beginner

Big teddy

Right leg

Cast on 15 sts with brown and light brown mix yarn and st/st 9 rows, starting with p row.
Break yarn, keep stitches on a spare needle or a stitch holder.

Left leg

Follow the instructions given for the right leg, but do not break off the yarn. With right side facing, place the right leg on the left side of the left leg on the same needle and continue.
Row 10: k7, yf, sl1, yb, turn, sl1, p to end.
Row 11: k across all sts to connect the two legs (30).

Row 12: p7, yb, sl1, yf, turn, sl1, k to end.
Row 13: p.
Row 14: k21, yf, sl1, yb, turn, sl1, p15, yb, sl1, yf, turn, k to end.
Rows 15–21: st/st.
Row 22: (k2tog) to end (15).
Row 23: p.
Row 24: kf/b in each st (30).
Rows 25–34: st/st.
Row 35: (p2tog) to end (15).
Break yarn, draw through sts, pull tightly and fasten off.

Arms: make two

Cast on 8 sts with brown and light brown mix yarn and st/st 9 rows, starting with a k row.
Break yarn, draw through sts, pull tightly and fasten off.

Ears: make two

Cast on 10 sts with brown and light brown mix yarn and p 1 row.
Break yarn, draw through sts, pull tightly and fasten off.

Muzzle

Cast on 14 sts with beige yarn and p 1 row. Break yarn, draw through sts, pull tightly and fasten off.

Scarf

Cast on 4 sts with dark red yarn and work an i-cord for 12cm (4¾in). Break yarn, draw through sts, pull tightly and fasten off.

To make up

Make up as for the small teddy.

Cosy snowmen

Instructions

Body and head

Cast on 10 sts with white yarn.
Row 1: p.
Row 2: kf/b in each st (20).
Rows 3–11: st/st.
Row 12 (shape neck): (k2tog) to end (10).
Row 13: p.
Row 14: (kf/b) to end (20).
Rows 15–23: st/st.
Row 24: (k2tog) to end (10).
Break yarn, draw through sts, pull tightly and fasten off.

Hat

Cast on 22 sts with multi-coloured yarn.
Rows 1–8: st/st, starting with a k row.
Row 9: k1, (k2tog, k1) to end (15).
Rows 10–12: st/st.
Row 13: (k2tog) to last st, k1 (8).
Break yarn, draw through sts, pull tightly and fasten off.

Scarf

Cast on 3 sts with multi-coloured yarn and work an i-cord for 10cm (4in). Break yarn, draw through sts, pull tightly and fasten off.

To make up

Sew the body seam, leaving a gap at the base. Roll the stuffing into two small balls and stuff the head and body, avoiding the neck area. With the cast-on end of yarn, work a gathering thread along the cast-on edge and sew up the rest of the base seam. Work a gathering thread around the neck at row 12, draw up tightly and fasten off.

Sew the seam of the hat and attach it to the head.

Using dark brown fingering (4-ply) yarn or two strands taken from DK (8-ply) yarn, embroider each eye with a French knot and each eyebrow with a backstitch (see page 22).

Materials

DK (8-ply) yarn: 5g (⅙oz), white

DK (8-ply) yarn: small amount of multi-coloured

Fingering (4-ply) yarn: small amount of dark brown and pink or two strands taken from dark brown and pink DK (8-ply) yarn

Stuffing

Size

6cm (2¼in) tall

Difficulty level

Beginner

Embroider the nose and mouth with a French knot, using pink fingering (4-ply) yarn or two strands taken from pink DK (8-ply) yarn. Sew in the ends of the scarf and tie the scarf around the neck.

Awesome aeroplanes

Instructions

Main body

Starting with the tail, cast on 6 sts with blue yarn.

Row 1: p.
Row 2: kf/b in each st (12).
Row 3: p.
Row 4: (k1, kf/b) to end (18).
Row 5: p.
Row 6: (k2, kf/b) to end (24).
Rows 7–16: st/st.
Rows 17–18: change to light blue yarn and st/st.
Row 19: (p2, p2tog) to end (18).
Rows 20–22: st/st.
Row 23: (p2, p2tog) to last 2 sts, p2 (14).
Rows 24–26: st/st.
Row 27: (p2tog) to end (7).
Break yarn, draw through sts, pull tightly and fasten off.

Wings: make two

Cast on 8 sts with light blue yarn.
Rows 1–4: st/st, starting with a k row.
Row 5: skpo, k to end (7).
Row 6: p to last 2 sts, p2tog (6).
Row 7: skpo, k to end (5).
Row 8: k for fold line. (This is the front edge.)
Row 9: kf/b, k to end (6).
Row 10: p to last st, pf/b (7).
Row 11: kf/b, k to end (8).
Rows 12–15: st/st.
Cast off.

Tail wings: make three

With light blue yarn cast on 8 sts.
Rows 1–2: st/st, starting with a k row.
Row 3: skpo, k to last 2 sts, k2tog (6).
Row 4: p.
Row 5: as row 3 (4).
Break yarn, draw through sts, pull tightly and fasten off.

Propeller

Cast on 12 sts with aqua blue yarn.
Rows 1–4: st/st, starting with a k row.
Row 5: p for fold line.
Rows 6–9: st/st, starting with a p row.
Cast off.

Centre of the propeller

Cast on 6 sts with red yarn.
Break yarn, draw through sts, pull tightly and fasten off.

Materials

Blue aeroplane:

DK (8-ply) yarn: 4g (⅛oz) each of blue and light blue

DK (8-ply) yarn: small amounts of aqua blue and red

Stuffing

Size

7cm (2¾in) long

Difficulty level

Beginner

To make up

Sew the body seam, leaving a gap for stuffing. Stuff and close the seam. Fold each wing piece, each tail wing piece and the propeller in half with right sides out and sew the seams without stuffing. Attach them to the body, using the picture for guidance. Sew the red centre of the propeller in place at the front of the aeroplane.

Colourful chameleons

Instructions

Body and tail

Starting at the tail, cast on 3 sts with green or khaki yellow yarn.
Rows 1–20: work an i-cord.
Work in st/st from this point on.
Row 21: cast on 1 st, p2, pf/b (5).
Row 22: kf/b, k3, kf/b (7).
Row 23: pf/b, p to last st, pf/b (9).
Row 24: kf/b, k to last st, kf/b (11).
Row 25: as row 23 (13).
Row 26: as row 24 (15).
Row 27: as row 23 (17).
Row 28: k.
Row 29: p.
Row 30: kf/b, k to last st, kf/b (19).
Rows 31–35: st/st.
Row 36: (k2, k2tog) to last 3 sts, k3 (15).
Rows 37–39: st/st.
Cast off.

Head

Cast on 30 sts with green or khaki yellow yarn.
Rows 1–4: st/st, starting with a k row.
Row 5: k13, (k2tog) twice, k13 (28).
Row 6: p10, (p2tog) four times, p10 (24).
Row 7: k11, k2tog, k11 (23).
Rows 8–10: st/st.
Row 11: (k2, k2tog) to last 3 sts, k3 (18).
Row 12: p.
Row 13: (k1, k2tog) to end (12).
Break yarn, draw through sts, pull tightly and fasten off.

Eyes: make two

Cast on 10 sts with green or khaki yellow yarn and p 1 row. Break yarn, draw through sts, pull tightly and fasten off.

Tummy

Cast on 7 sts with light green yarn.
Rows 1–12: st/st, starting with a k row.
Row 13: skpo, k3, k2tog (5).
Rows 14–16: st/st.
Row 17: skpo, k1, k2tog (3).
Rows 18–20: st/st.
Row 21: k1, k2tog (2).
Row 22: p2tog and fasten off.

Front legs: make two

Cast on 4 sts with green or khaki yellow yarn and work an i-cord for 5 rows.
Row 6: k2, then work an i-cord for one more row on these 2 sts only, using another needle.
Pass the first stitch over the second stitch and fasten off.
Rejoin yarn to the remaining 2 sts and work an i-cord for two rows on these 2 sts only.
Pass the first stitch over the second stitch and fasten off.

Back legs: make two

Follow the instructions given for the front legs, except work an i-cord for 6 rows instead of 5 rows at the start.

To make up

Sew the tummy and the top of the body together, leaving a gap for stuffing. Stuff and close the seam.

Materials

DK (8-ply) yarn:
    10g (⅓oz), green or khaki yellow

DK (8-ply) yarn: small amounts of light green for the tummy, brown for the mouth and yellow or green for the stripes

Stuffing

Size

11cm (4¼in) long, including the tail

Difficulty level

Intermediate

To create the bump on the top of the head, pinch together about 1cm (½in) of the cast-on edge on the top of the head and sew the seam. Starting at the fasten-off end, sew the head seam. Leave the cast-on end open. Stuff the head. Attach the cast-on edge of the head to the body. Attach the front and back legs.

Attach the eyes to the head, using the picture for guidance. Using dark brown fingering (4-ply) yarn or two strands taken from dark brown DK (8-ply) yarn, embroider the centre of each eye with a French knot. Embroider the mouth with brown DK (8-ply) yarn and backstitch. Embroider the stripes with yellow or green DK (8-ply) yarn and backstitch. Coil the tail and secure it with a few stitches to shape.

Little Red Riding Hood & the wolf

Instructions

Little Red Riding Hood

Body and head

Cast on 6 sts with red yarn.
Row 1: p.
Row 2: kf/b in each st (12).
Row 3: p.
Row 4: (k1, kf/b) to end (18).
Row 5: k for fold line.
Rows 6–13: st/st, starting with a k row.
Row 14: (k1, k2tog) to end (12).
Change to skin colour yarn.
Row 15: p.
Row 16: k4, (kf/b) four times, k4 (16).
Rows 17–19: st/st.
Row 20: k3, (k2tog, k1) three times, k4 (13).
Rows 21–22: st/st.
Row 23: p1, (p2tog, p1) to end (9).
Break yarn, draw through sts, pull tightly and fasten off.

Hood

Cast on 20 sts with red yarn.
Rows 1–4: st/st, starting with a k row.
Row 5: (k2tog) to end (10).
Row 6: p.
Row 7: kf/b to end (20).
Rows 8–14: st/st.
Cast off.

To make up

Sew up the body and head and flatten the base, following the instructions on pages 16–18. Work a gathering thread around the eye line. Using golden brown DK (8-ply) yarn, make loops for the hair with backstitch, leaving a loop every other stitch. Embroider each eye with a French knot and brown DK (8-ply) yarn. Create a nose by backstitching the same spot three times using skin colour DK (8-ply) yarn. Fold the hood in half across the cast-off edge and and sew the cast-off edge together to form the top of the hood. Place the hood on the head and secure with a few stitches.

Wolf

Body and head

Starting with the base, cast on 6 sts with grey yarn.
Row 1: p.
Row 2: kf/b in each st (12).
Row 3: p.
Row 4: (k1, kf/b) to end (18).
Join in white yarn.
Row 5: p4 white, p10 grey, p4 white.
Rows 6–15: keeping the colours correct, st/st.
Row 16: (k1, k2tog, k1) white, k2 grey, (k2tog, k2) twice in grey, (k1, k2tog, k1) white (14).
Row 17: cast on 4 sts in white, keeping the colours correct, p to end (18).

Row 18: cast on 4 sts in white, keeping the colours correct, k to end (22).
Row 19: keeping the colours correct, p.
Break off white yarn, continue with grey yarn only.
Row 20: k.
Row 21: p.
Row 22: cast off 5 sts, k to end (17).
Row 23: cast off 5 sts, p to end (12).
Cast off.

Materials

Little Red Riding Hood:
DK (8-ply) yarn: 5g (1/6oz), red

DK (8-ply) yarn: small amounts of skin colour, golden brown and dark brown

Stuffing

Wolf:
DK (8-ply) yarn: small amounts of grey, white, brown and black

Stuffing

Size
Little Red Riding Hood: 5cm (2in) tall

Wolf: 6cm (2¼in) tall

Difficulty level
Beginner

Tail

Cast on 8 sts with grey yarn.
Rows 1–8: st/st, starting with a p row.
Row 9: (p2tog) to end (4).
Break yarn, draw through sts, pull tightly and fasten off.

Ears: make two

Cast on 5 sts with grey yarn.
Row 1: p2tog, p1, p2tog (3).

Row 2: k1, k2tog (2).
Pass the first stitch over the second stitch and fasten off.
Hide the fasten-off end of yarn inside the sts.

Nose

Cast on 6 sts with brown yarn.
Break yarn, draw through sts, pull tightly and fasten off.

To make up

Sew the seams, stuff and flatten the base as shown on pages 16–18. Attach the ears, the tail and the nose. Embroider each eye with a French knot using black DK (8-ply) yarn.

Three little pigs

Instructions

Pigs: make three

Body and head

Starting with the base, cast on 7 sts with pink yarn.
Row 1: p.
Row 2: kf/b in each st (14).
Row 3: p.
Row 4: (k1, kf/b) to end (21).
Rows 5–15: st/st.
Row 16: (k1, k2tog, k1) to last st, k1 (16).
Row 17: p.
Row 18: k1, (k2tog, k1) to end (11).
Break yarn, draw through sts, pull tightly and fasten off.

Ears: make two

Cast on 4 sts with pink yarn.
Row 1: p.
Row 2: skpo, k2tog (2).
Row 3: p2tog and fasten off.

Snout

Cast on 10 sts with pink yarn. Break yarn, draw through sts, pull tightly and fasten off.

Tail

Make 6 chains with crochet hook and pink yarn. Fasten off.

To make up

Sew the body seam, stuff and flatten the base as shown on pages 16–18. Attach the ears, snout and tail. Using dark brown fingering (4-ply) yarn or two strands taken from dark brown DK (8-ply) yarn, embroider each eye with a French knot and the nostrils with backstitch (see page 22).

Materials

DK (8-ply) yarn: 10g (1/3oz), pink

Fingering (4-ply) yarn: small amount of dark brown, or two strands taken from dark brown DK (8-ply) yarn

Stuffing

Additional Equipment

3mm (UK 11, US C/2 or D/3) crochet hook

Size

4cm (1½in) tall

Difficulty level

Beginner

Snuggly pandas

Instructions

Body and head

Starting with the base, cast on 8 sts with pink or light blue yarn.

Row 1: p.

Row 2: kf/b in each st (16).

Row 3: p.

Row 4: (k1, kf/b) to end (24).

Row 5: (p2, k1) to end.

Row 6: (p1, k2) to end.

Rows 7–16: repeat rows 5 and 6 five times.

Rows 17–26: change to white yarn and, starting with a p row, st/st.

Row 27: (p2, p2tog) to end (18).

Row 28: (k1, k2tog) to end (12).

Break yarn, draw through sts, pull tightly and fasten off.

Ears: make two

Cast on 9 sts with black yarn. Break yarn, draw through sts, pull tightly and fasten off.

Muzzle

Cast on 10 sts with white yarn. Break yarn, draw through sts, pull tightly and fasten off.

Eyes: make two

Cast on 10 sts with black fingering (4-ply) yarn. Break yarn, draw through sts, pull tightly and fasten off (see page 20).

Arms: make two

Cast on 6 sts with black yarn and work an i-cord for 5 rows (see page 21). Break yarn, draw through sts, pull tightly and fasten off.

Scarf

Cast on 4 sts with light green or light yellow yarn and work an i-cord for 16cm (6¼in). Break yarn, draw through sts, pull tightly and fasten off.

Materials

DK (8-ply) yarn: small amounts of pink, light blue, black, white, light green, light yellow and brown

Fingering (4-ply) yarn: small amount of black

Stuffing

Size

6cm (2¼in) tall

Difficulty level

Beginner

To make up

Sew the body seam, leaving a gap for stuffing. Stuff and close the seam. Attach the arms, ears, and eyes. Attach the muzzle. Using two strands of white DK (8-ply) yarn, embroider the centre of each eye with a French knot (see page 22). Embroider the nose and mouth using black or brown yarn and backstitch. Attach the scarf. Use the picture for guidance.

Bouncing balls

Instructions

Baseball

Make two pieces the same: one with cream yarn, one with light blue yarn.

Cast on 8 sts.

Row 1: kf/b, k to last st, kf/b (10).
Row 2: kf/b, p to last st, kf/b (12).
Row 3: kf/b, k to last st, kf/b (14).
Row 4: kf/b, p to last st, kf/b (16).
Row 5: kf/b, k to last st, kf/b (18).
Row 6: k2, p to last 2 sts, k2.
Row 7: k.
Row 8: as row 6.
Row 9: k.
Row 10: as row 6.
Row 11: k2tog, k to last 2 sts, k2tog (16).
Row 12: k2, p to last 2 sts, k2.
Row 13: k.
Row 14: k2, p to last 2 sts, k2.
Row 15: k2tog, k to last 2 sts, k2tog (14).
Row 16: k2, p to last 2 sts, k2.
Row 17: k.
Row 18: k2, p to last 2 sts, k2.
Row 19: k2tog, k to last 2 sts, k2tog (12).
Row 20: k2, p to last 2 sts, k2.
Row 21: k.
Rows 22–41: repeat rows 20 and 21 ten times.
Row 42: as row 20.
Row 43: kf/b, k to last st, kf/b (14).
Row 44: k2, p to last 2 sts, k2.
Row 45: k.
Row 46: k2, p to last 2 sts, k2.
Row 47: kf/b, k to last st, kf/b (16).
Row 48: k2, p to last 2 sts, k2.
Row 49: k.
Row 50: k2, p to last 2 sts, k2.

Row 51: kf/b, k to last st, kf/b (18).
Row 52: k2, p to last 2 sts, k2.
Row 53: k.
Row 54: k2, p to last 2 sts, k2.
Row 55: k.
Row 56: k2, p to last 2 sts, k2.
Row 57: kf/b, k to last st, kf/b (20).
Row 58: k2, p to last 2 sts, k2.
Row 59: k2tog, k to last 2 sts, k2tog (18).
Row 60: k2tog, p to last 2 sts, k2tog (16).
Row 61: k2tog, k to last 2 sts, k2tog (14).
Row 62: k2tog, p to last 2 sts, k2tog (12).
Row 63: k2tog, k to last 2 sts, k2tog (10).
Row 64: k2tog, p to last 2 sts, k2tog (8).
Cast off.

To make up

Mark the centre of each edge on both knitted pieces. Using the diagram for guidance, match the centre of one short edge (A) on one knitted piece to the centre of one long edge (A) on the other knitted piece. Match the other edges in the same way and sew the seam, leaving a gap for stuffing. Stuff and close the seam.

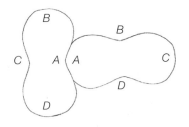

Materials

Baseball:

DK (8-ply) yarn: 10g (1/3oz), cream

DK (8-ply) yarn: 10g (1/3oz), light blue

Stuffing

Basketball:

DK (8-ply) yarn: 10g (1/3oz), light brown

DK (8-ply) yarn: small amount of dark brown

Stuffing

Size

8cm (3¼in) diameter

Difficulty level

Beginner

Basketball

Follow the pattern given for the baseball, using light brown yarn. Add the embroidery with chain stitches using dark brown DK (8-ply) yarn (see page 23).

Scrumptious cupcakes

Instructions

The cupcakes can be knitted flat, if you prefer. Simply continue knitting flat in st/st after row 8, and sew the seam at the end.

Strawberry cupcake

Starting with the base, cast on 7 sts loosely with white yarn.
Row 1: kf/b in each st (14).
Row 2: p.
Row 3: (k1, kf/b) to end (21).
Row 4: p.
Row 5: (k2, kf/b) to end (28).
Row 6: p.
Row 7: (k3, kf/b) to end (35).
Row 8: k for fold line, inc one st at the end of the row (36).
Divide sts equally on 3 needles and start working in rounds.
Rounds 9–20: (k2, p1) to end.
Round 21: p for the edge.
Break off white yarn and change to beige yarn.
Rounds 22–32: k.
Round 33: (k2, k2tog) to end (27).
Rounds 34–35: k.
Round 36: (k2, k2tog) to last 3 sts, k3 (21).
Break yarn, draw through sts, pull tightly and fasten off.

Whipped cream

Cast on 20 sts with white fleecy, chunky or bouclé yarn and 4mm (UK 8, US 6) needles and k1 row.
Row 2: (p2tog) to end (10).
Break yarn, draw through sts, pull tightly and fasten off.

Strawberry

Cast on 12 sts with green yarn.
Row 1: p.
Join in red yarn.
Row 2: (k3 green, k1 red) to end.
Row 3: (p1 red, p3 green) to end.
Break off green yarn and continue in red yarn only.
Rows 4–7: st/st.
Row 8: (k2, k2tog) to end (9).
Break yarn, draw through sts, pull tightly and fasten off.
Sew the seam from the fasten-off end and stuff.

To make up

Starting at the fasten-off end of the whipped cream, sew the side seam. Starting at the fasten-off end of the strawberry, sew the seam, leaving a gap for stuffing. Stuff and close the seam. Work a gathering thread along the cast-on edge, pull tightly and fasten off. Embroider dots on the strawberry with two strands taken from white DK (8-ply) yarn. See the picture for guidance. Sew the cupcake seam, leaving a gap for stuffing. Stuff and close the seam. Attach the whipped cream and the strawberry securely to the top of the cupcake.

Materials

Strawberry cupcake:

DK (8-ply) yarn: 4g (1/8oz) each of beige and white

Fleecy, chunky yarn or bouclé yarn: small amounts of white

Note: If the bouclé yarn is very fine, you could knit with two strands of the yarn held together.

DK (8-ply) yarn: small amounts of red and green

Stuffing

Cupcake with frosting:

DK (8-ply) yarn: 4g (1/8oz) white

DK (8-ply) yarn: 3g (1/10oz) beige and pink

DK (8-ply) yarn: small amount of dark brown

Stuffing

Additional equipment

A pair of 4mm (UK 8, US 6) knitting needles

Size

Strawberry cupcake: 5cm (2in) diameter, 8cm (8¼in) tall

Cupcake with frosting: 5cm (2in) diameter, 6cm (2¼in) tall

Difficulty level

Beginner

Cupcake with frosting

Follow the instructions for the strawberry cupcake until round 30.
Round 31: (k2, k2tog) to end (27).
Round 32: k.
Round 33: (k2, k2tog) to last 3 sts, k3 (21).
Round 34: (k1, k2tog) to end (14).

Break yarn, draw through sts, pull tightly and fasten off.

Frosting

Cast on 9 sts with pink yarn.
Row 1: (k2, p1) to end.
Row 2: (k1, p2) to end.
Repeat rows 1 and 2 until the piece measures 14cm (5½in).
Cast off.

To make up

Make up the cupcake with frosting as for the strawberry cupcake. Sew the side seams of the frosting, roll the piece from one end and shape. Secure it to the top of the cupcake. For the chocolate sprinkles, embroider dots on the cream with dark brown DK (8-ply) yarn. See the picture for guidance.

Choo-choo train

Instructions

The engine is knitted from the left panel and moves on to the roof panel, the right panel and the base panel. The front and back panels (knitted in green yarn) are created from stitches picked up from the roof edges. The very front panel, which creates the front of the engine (knitted in beige yarn) is created from stitches picked up from the main part of the engine. Refer to the marking threads throughout the pattern.

Engine

Cast on 14 sts with beige yarn.
Rows 1–4: (left panel) st/st, starting with a p row.
Row 5: k for fold line.
Join in green yarn.
Row 6: k5 green, turn. Leave the beige sts on a stitch holder and work on the 5 sts in green yarn first.
Rows 7–14: st/st, starting with a p row.
Row 15: k for fold line. Leave a red marking thread at the beginning of the row and a blue marking thread at the end of the row.
Rows 16–24 (roof panel): st/st, starting with a k row.
Row 25: k for fold line. Leave a red marking thread at the beginning of the row and a blue marking thread at the end of the row.
Rows 26–33 (right panel): st/st, starting with a k row. Leave the sts on a second stitch holder.
Back panel: with green yarn and the right side facing, pick up 7 sts between the two red marking threads, turn and st/st 12 rows, starting with a p row (WS). Cast off.
Front panel: with green yarn and

the right side facing, pick up 7 sts between the two blue marking threads, turn and st/st 8 rows, starting with a p row (WS). Cast off.
Go back to the beige sts you left at row 6, on stitch holder 1. With right side facing, rejoin beige yarn and k to end (9). Leave a yellow marking thread at the end of the row.
St/st 6 more rows, starting with a p row. Do not break the yarn. With right side facing, transfer the 5 sts on stitch holder 2 to the right side of the beige stitches you have just been working on. The previous row number is used from this point.
Row 34 (right panel) (WS): with beige yarn, p across the row to connect the green and beige sts (14). Leave a yellow marking thread at the beginning of the row.
Row 35: p for fold line.
Rows 36–39: st/st, starting with a p row.
Row 40: k for fold line.
Rows 41–49 (base panel): st/st, starting with a k row. Cast off.
Front panel of the beige main body piece: with beige yarn and the right side facing, pick up 7 sts between the two yellow marking threads, turn and st/st 4 rows, starting with a p row (WS). Cast off.

Front box

This box has one open end. The open end will be attached to the green front panel of the engine.
Cast on 9 sts with pink yarn.
Rows 1–5: st/st, starting with a k row.
Row 6: k for fold line.
Rows 7–11: st/st, starting with a k row.

Materials

DK (8-ply) yarn: small amounts of beige, green, pink, cream, brown, dark pink, blue, orange and yellow

DK (8-ply) yarn: small amounts of red, blue, and yellow for stitch markers

Stuffing

Additional equipment

Two spare needles or stitch holders

Size

Train, 5cm (2in) wide, 21cm (8¼in) long with all carriages connected

Difficulty level

Intermediate

Row 12: cast on 5 sts, p these sts, k to end for fold line (14).
Rows 13–17: st/st, starting with a k row.
Row 18: cast off 5 sts, k to end for fold line (9).
Rows 19–23: st/st, starting with a k row. Cast off.

Wheels: make eight

Cast on 3 sts with cream yarn and work in g-st for 22 rows. Change to brown yarn and work in g-st for 22 rows. Cast off.

Roof

Cast on 10 sts with dark pink yarn and work in g-st for 13 rows. Cast off.

Chimney

Cast on 6 sts with dark pink yarn and work an i-cord for 3 rows. Break yarn, draw through sts, pull tightly and fasten off.

Windows: make two

Cast on 8 sts with dark pink yarn. Break yarn, draw through sts, pull tightly and fasten off.

Carriages: make two

Cast on 12 sts with blue or orange yarn.

Rows 1–7: st/st, starting with a k row.

Row 8: cast on 6 sts, p these sts, k to end for fold line (18).

Row 9: cast on 6 sts, k to end (24).

Rows 10–17: st/st, starting with a p row.

Row 18: cast off 6 sts, k to end for fold line (18).

Row 19: cast off 6 sts, k to end (12).

Rows 20–25: st/st, starting with a p row.

Row 26: k for fold line.

Rows 27–35: st/st, starting with a k row.

Cast off.

Connecting pieces: make two

Cast on 2 sts with yellow yarn and work an i-cord for 6 rows. Pass the first stitch over the second stitch and fasten off.

To make up

Sew the seams of the engine, leaving a gap for stuffing. Stuff and close the seam. Sew the seams of the front box and stuff. Attach the open end of the front box to the green front panel of the engine. Attach the roof, chimney and windows.

Sew the seams of each carriage, leaving a gap for stuffing. Stuff and close the seam.

Starting at the cream coloured end, roll up each wheel piece and secure with a few stitches using brown yarn. Attach the wheels to the engine and carriages – see the picture for guidance. Attach the connecting pieces to connect the carriages together.

Cute cats and marvellous mice

Instructions

Cat

Body and head

Starting with the base, cast on 7 sts with beige or honey-yellow yarn.
Row 1: p.
Row 2: kf/b in each st (14).
Row 3: p.
Row 4: (k1, kf/b) to end (21).
Rows 5–15: st/st.
Row 16: (k1, k2tog, k1) to last st, k1 (16).
Row 17: p.
Row 18: k1, (k2tog, k1) to end (11).
Break yarn, draw through sts, pull tightly and fasten off.

Muzzle

Cast on 14 sts with white yarn.
Next row: p2, (p2tog, p2) to end (11).
Break yarn, draw through sts, pull tightly and fasten off.

Ears: make two

Cast on 4 sts with beige or honey-yellow yarn.
Row 1: (p2tog) twice (2).
Row 2: skpo and fasten off.

Tail

Cast on 2 sts with beige or honey-yellow yarn and work an i-cord for 15 rows (see page 21). Pass the first stitch over the second stitch and fasten off.

To make up

Sew the body seam, stuff and flatten the base as shown on pages 16–18. Hide the yarn ends of each ear and attach the ears to the body. Attach the muzzle with the purl side out. Work a gathering thread around the centre of the muzzle to shape. Using two strands taken from dark brown DK (8-ply) yarn, embroider the eyes and the nose with French knots and the mouth with backstitch (see page 22). Using two strands taken from brown DK (8-ply) yarn, embroider the whiskers with backstitch. Embroider the stripes using brown DK (8-ply) yarn and backstitch. Attach the tail.

Mouse

Body and head

Cast on 6 sts with white yarn.
Row 1: p.
Row 2: kf/b in each st (12).
Rows 3–11: st/st.
Break yarn, draw through sts, pull tightly and fasten off.

Materials

DK (8-ply) yarn: small amounts of beige, honey-yellow, white, dark brown and brown

Stuffing

Additional equipment

3mm (UK 11, US C/2 or D/3) crochet hook

Size

Cat: 4cm (1½in) tall

Mouse: 2cm (¾in) tall

Note: the mouse is tiny. Please take care if you give it to a young child.

Difficulty level

Beginner

Ears: make two

Cast on 3 sts with white yarn. Break yarn, draw through sts, pull tightly and fasten off.

Tail

Make 10 chains with a crochet hook and white yarn. Fasten off.

To make up

Sew the body seam, stuff and flatten the base as shown on pages 16–18. Attach the ears and tail. Using two strands taken from dark brown DK (8-ply) yarn, embroider the eyes and the nose with French knots and the mouth with backstitch (see page 22). Using two strands taken from brown DK (8-ply) yarn, embroider the whiskers with backstitch.

Balancing baby clowns

Instructions

Body, head and legs

Right leg

Cast on 7 sts with lilac yarn or pink yarn and st/st 5 rows, starting with a p row.

Break yarn and keep the sts on a spare needle or a holder.

Left leg

Follow the instructions given for the right leg, but do not break off the yarn. With right side facing, place the right leg on the left side of the left leg on the same needle and continue.

Row 6: k6, k2tog, k6 (13).
Rows 7–11: st/st.
Row 12: k1, (k2tog, k1) to end (9).
Change to skin colour yarn.
Row 13: p.
Row 14: k2, kf/b, k3, kf/b, k2 (11).
Rows 15–19: st/st.
Row 20: (k2, k2tog) to last 3 sts, k3 (9).

Break yarn, draw through sts, pull tightly and fasten off.

Hat

Cast on 13 sts with lilac yarn or pink yarn.

Rows 1–5: st/st, starting with a k row.
Row 6: (p2tog) to last st, p1 (7).
Row 7: k.

Break yarn, draw through sts, pull tightly and fasten off.

Arms: make two

Cast on 2 sts with lilac or pink yarn and work an i-cord for 4 rows (see page 21). Break yarn, draw through sts, pull tightly and fasten off.

To make up

Starting at the fasten-off end, sew the head and body seam, leaving a gap for stuffing. Stuff, avoiding the neck area and close the seam. Work a gathering thread around the neck with skin colour yarn, pull tightly and fasten off. Sew each leg seam, leaving a gap for stuffing. Stuff and close the seam.

Attach the arms. Sew the seam on the hat and attach it to the head. Attach a length of white fleecy, chunky or bouclé yarn around the neck. Embroider the nose by backstitching on the same spot three times with skin colour yarn. Embroider each eye with a French knot using dark brown fingering (4-ply) yarn or two strands taken from dark brown DK (8-ply) yarn.

Ball

Cast on 24 sts with yellow yarn.
Row 1: (p4 yellow, p4 light green, p4 light blue) twice.
Rows 2–11: keeping the colours correct, st/st.

Break yarn, draw through sts, pull tightly and fasten off.

To make up

Starting at the fasten-off end of the ball, sew the seam and stuff. Work a gathering thread along the cast-on edge, pull tightly and fasten off to shape the ball.

Materials

DK (8-ply) yarn: 4g (1/8oz), lilac or pink

DK (8-ply) yarn: small amount of skin colour

DK (8-ply) yarn: small amounts of yellow, light green and light blue for the ball

Fleecy, chunky yarn or bouclé yarn: small amount of white

Fingering (4-ply) yarn: small amount of dark brown or two strands taken from dark brown DK (8-ply) yarn

Stuffing

Additional equipment

A spare needle or stitch holder

Size

Baby: 6cm (2¼in) tall

Ball: 4cm (1½in) tall

Difficulty level

Intermediate

Doggy buddies

Instructions

Blue dog

Head

Cast on 10 sts with beige yarn.
Row 1: p.
Row 2: kf/b in each st (20).
Rows 3–13: st/st.
Row 14: (k1, k2tog) to last 2 sts, k2 (14).
Break yarn, draw through sts, pull tightly and fasten off.

Feet: make two

Starting with the back, cast on 8 sts with beige yarn.
Row 1: p.
Row 2: k.
Row 3: (p1, pf/b) to last 2 sts, p2 (11).
Rows 4–7: st/st.
Row 8: k2, k2tog, k3, k2tog, k2 (9).
Break yarn, draw through sts, pull tightly and fasten off.

Arms: make two

Cast on 8 sts with beige yarn and st/st 6 rows, starting with a k row.
Row 7: (k2tog) to end (4).
Break yarn, draw through sts, pull tightly and fasten off.

Ears: make two

Cast on 8 sts with brown yarn.
Row 1: p.
Row 2: k.
Row 3: (p1, pf/b) to last 2 sts, p2 (11).
Rows 4–5: st/st.

Row 6: k2, k2tog, k3, k2tog, k2 (9).
Break yarn, draw through sts, pull tightly and fasten off.

Body and legs

*Cast on 10 sts with dark blue yarn and st/st 3 rows, starting with a p row. Break yarn and keep the sts on a spare needle.
Repeat from *, but do not break yarn. Place the first piece on to the left side of the same needle and continue.
Row 4: (kf/b, k8, kf/b) twice, working across both pieces (24).
Change to light blue yarn.
Rows 5–15: st/st.
Row 16: (k2, k2tog) to end (18).
Break yarn, draw through sts, pull tightly and fasten off.

To make up

Starting at the fasten-off end, sew the head seam, leaving a gap for stuffing. Stuff and close the seam. Sew each leg seam, leaving the foot ends open and stuff the legs. Sew the seam at the back of the body, leaving a gap for stuffing. Stuff the body and close the seam. Sew each foot seam, leaving a gap for stuffing. Stuff and close the seam. Attach the feet to the legs. Sew the arm seams and stuff; attach the arms to the body. Sew the seams of each ear, without stuffing and attach to the head. Attach the head to the body. With brown DK (8-ply) yarn, embroider each eye with a French knot and a nose and mouth with backstitch.

Materials

DK (8-ply) yarn: 5g ($\frac{1}{6}$oz), beige for each dog

DK (8-ply) yarn: small amounts of brown, light blue, dark blue, light pink and dark pink

Stuffing

Additional equipment

Spare needle or stitch holder

Size

Boy: 8cm (3¼in) tall

Girl: 7cm (2¾in) tall

Difficulty level

Beginner

Pink dog

Head

Cast on 9 sts with beige yarn.
Row 1: p.
Row 2: kf/b in each st (18).
Rows 3–10: st/st.
Row 11: (p1, p2tog) to end (12).
Break yarn, draw through sts, pull tightly and fasten off.

Feet: make two

Cast on 7 sts with beige yarn.
Row 1: p.
Row 2: k.
Row 3: p1, (pf/b, p1) to end (10).
Row 4: k.
Row 5: p.
Row 6: k2, (k2tog, k2) to end (8).
Break yarn, draw through sts, pull tightly and fasten off.

Arms: make two

Cast on 5 sts with beige yarn and work an i-cord for 5 rows.

Row 6: k2tog, k1, k2tog (3). Break yarn, draw through sts, pull tightly and fasten off.

Body and legs

*Cast on 8 sts with dark pink yarn and st/st 3 rows, starting with a p row. Break yarn and keep the sts on a spare needle.

Repeat from * but do not break yarn. Place the first piece on to the left side of the same needle and continue.

Row 4: (kf/b, k6, kf/b) twice, working across both pieces (20). Change to light pink yarn.

Rows 5–13: st/st.

Row 14: (k2, k2tog) to end (15). Break yarn, draw through sts, pull tightly and fasten off.

Ears: make two

Cast on 8 sts with brown yarn.

Row 1: p.

Row 2: k.

Row 3: p2 (p1, pf/b, p1) to end (10).

Row 4: k.

Row 5: p2, (p2tog, p2) to end (8). Break yarn, draw through sts, pull tightly and fasten off.

To make up

Make up as given for the blue dog, except when attaching the arms: the i-cord arms can be sewn directly to the body and do not need seaming or stuffing.

Cheeky monkeys

Instructions

Head

Cast on 7 sts with brown yarn.
Row 1: kf/b in each st (14).
Join in beige yarn.
Row 2: p4 brown, p5 beige, p5 brown.
Row 3: keeping the colours correct, k.
Row 4: p3 brown, p7 beige, p4 brown.
Row 5: keeping the colours correct, k.
Break off brown yarn and continue with beige yarn only.
Row 6: p.
Row 7: k.
Row 8: (p1, p2tog) to last 2 sts, p2tog (9).
Break yarn, draw through sts, pull tightly and fasten off.

Note: the head piece is not symmetrical. As the seam is at the back, this doesn't really matter.

Body

Starting with the neck, cast on 7 sts with brown yarn.
Row 1: p.
Row 2: (kf/b) seven times (14).
Rows 3–5: st/st.
Row 6: k3, kf/b, k to last 4 sts, kf/b, k3 (16).
Rows 7–15: st/st.
Row 16: (k1, k2tog, k1) to end (12).
Break yarn, draw through sts, pull tightly and fasten off.

Ears: make two

Cast on 7 sts with beige yarn. Break yarn, draw through sts, pull tightly and fasten off.

Arms: make two

Cast on 5 sts with brown yarn and work an i-cord for 4 rows (see page 21). Change to beige yarn and work the same cord for 2 more rows. Break yarn, draw through sts, pull tightly and fasten off.

Legs: make two

Cast on 6 sts with brown yarn and work an i-cord for 5 rows. Change to beige yarn and work the same cord for 2 more rows.
Break yarn, draw through sts, pull tightly and fasten off.

Tail

Cast on 2 sts with brown yarn and work an i-cord for 4cm (1½in). Pass the first stitch over the second stitch and fasten off.

Banana

Cast on 2 sts with light yellow yarn and work an i-cord for 4 rows.
Break off light yellow yarn and join in a 30cm (11¾in) length of yellow yarn to one end of the i-cord.
Using a crochet hook, * make 4 chains, fasten off and thread the yarn through a sewing needle.
Hide the yarn end in the chain. Repeat from * twice more.

To make up

Sew the body seam, leaving a gap for stuffing. Stuff and close the

Materials

DK (8-ply) yarn: 5g (⅙oz), brown

DK (8-ply) yarn: small amounts of beige, yellow and light yellow

Fingering (4-ply) yarn: small amount of dark brown or two strands taken from dark brown DK (8-ply) yarn

Stuffing

Additional equipment

3mm (UK 11, US C/2 or D/3) crochet hook

Size

5cm (2in) sitting height

Difficulty level

Beginner

seam. Sew the head seam, leaving a gap for stuffing. Stuff and close the seam. Attach the head, legs, arms and tail to the body. Attach the ears to the head.

Using dark brown fingering (4-ply) yarn or two strands taken from dark brown DK (8-ply) yarn, embroider each eye with a French knot and embroider the nostrils and mouth with backstitch. Attach the banana to the hands.

Yellow submarine

Instructions

Main body

Starting with the tail, cast on 6 sts with yellow yarn.
Rows 1–3: st/st, starting with a p row.
Row 4: kf/b in each st (12).
Row 5: p.
Row 6: (k1, kf/b) to end (18).
Row 7: p.
Row 8: (k2, kf/b) to end (24).
Rows 9–20: st/st.
Row 21: (p2, p2tog) to end (18).
Rows 22–24: st/st.
Row 25: (p1, p2tog) to end (12).
Rows 26–28: st/st.
Row 29: (p2tog) to end (6).
Break yarn, draw through sts, pull tightly and fasten off.

Top compartment

Cast on 7 sts with yellow yarn.
Row 1: kf/b in each st (14).
Row 2: k for edge.
Row 3: k.
Row 4: p.
Break yarn, draw through sts, pull tightly and fasten off.

Tail piece

Cast on 6 sts with light brown yarn and p 1 row.
Break yarn, draw through sts, pull tightly and fasten off.

Propellers: make three

Cast on 4 sts with light brown yarn.
Row 1: k.
Row 2: k.

Row 3: k1, skpo, k1 (3).
Row 4: k.
Row 5: k1, skpo (2).
Row 6: k.
Pass the first stitch over the second stitch and fasten off.

Tail fins: make two

Cast on 6 sts with yellow yarn.
Row 1: p.
Row 2: skpo, k2, k2tog (4).
Row 3: p.
Cast off.

Windows: make six

Cast on 9 sts with light blue yarn. Break yarn, draw through sts, pull tightly and fasten off.

Periscope

Cast on 3 sts with yellow yarn and work an i-cord for 2cm (¾in). Break yarn, draw through sts, pull tightly and fasten off.

To make up

Sew the body seam, leaving a gap for stuffing. Stuff and close the seam. Fold and seam the tail fins; attach the tail fins and the tail piece. Attach the propellers to the tail piece. Sew the seam and stuff the top compartment. Attach the top compartment.
Bend the top of the periscope and secure with a few stitches to shape. Attach to the top compartment. Sew three windows to each side of the main body.

Materials

DK (8-ply) yarn: 5g (¹⁄₆oz), yellow

DK (8-ply) yarn: small amounts of light brown and light blue

Stuffing

Size

7cm (2¾in) long

Difficulty level

Beginner

Nuts about squirrels

Instructions

Body

Starting with the base, cast on 6 sts with light brown yarn.
Row 1: p.
Row 2: kf/b in each st (12).
Row 3: p.
Row 4: (k1, kf/b) to end (18).
Row 5: p.
Join in white yarn.
Row 6: k8 light brown, k2 white, k8 light brown.
Row 7: p7 light brown, p4 white, p7 light brown.
Row 8: k6 light brown, k6 white, k6 light brown.
Rows 9–13: keeping the colours correct, st/st.
Row 14: keeping the colours correct (k2, k2tog) to last 2 sts, k2 (14).
Break off white yarn and continue with light brown only.
Row 15: (p2tog) to end (7).
Break yarn, draw through sts, pull tightly and fasten off.

Head

Cast on 6 sts with light brown yarn.
Row 1: p.
Row 2: kf/b in each st (12).
Row 3: p.
Row 4: (k1, kf/b) to end (18).
Rows 5–8: st/st.
Row 9: p2, (p2tog, p2) to end (14).
Row 10: (k2tog) to end (7).
Break yarn, draw through sts, pull tightly and fasten off.

Feet: make two

Cast on 6 sts with light brown yarn.
Rows 1–2: st/st, starting with a p row.
Row 3: p1, pf/b, p2, pf/b, p1 (8).
Rows 4–6: st/st.
Row 7: p1, p2tog, p2, p2tog, p1 (6).
Break yarn, draw through sts, pull tightly and fasten off.

Arms: make two

Cast on 5 sts with light brown yarn and work an i-cord for 4 rows (see page 21). Break yarn, draw through sts, pull tightly and fasten off.

Ears: make two

Cast on 5 sts with light brown yarn.
Row 1: p2tog, p1, p2tog (3).
Row 2: sl1, k2tog (2).
Pass the first stitch over the second stitch and fasten off.

Tail

Cut a horizontal slit in the middle of the piece of card. Wind light brown DK (8-ply) yarn around the card, seventy times. Secure the length of yarn with stitches sewn through the slit with cotton thread; sew from one end to the other and back twice more, to secure the yarn firmly in place. Cut the yarn at the outer edges and release the card. Trim to shape.

Materials

DK (8-ply) yarn: 10g (1/3oz), light brown

DK (8-ply) yarn: small amounts of white and dark brown

DK (8-ply) yarn: small amounts of brown and dark brown for the acorn

2.5 x 7cm (1 x 2¾in) piece of card

Stuffing

Cotton sewing thread

Size
7cm (2¾in) tall

Difficulty level
Beginner

Acorn

Cast on 6 sts with brown yarn.
Row 1: p.
Row 2: kf/b in each st (12).
Rows 3–7: st/st.
Change to dark brown yarn.
Rows 8–10: k.
Row 11: (k2tog) to end (6).
Break yarn, draw through sts, pull tightly and fasten off.

To make up

Sew the body seam, leaving a gap for stuffing. Stuff and close the seam. Sew the head seam, leaving a gap for stuffing. Stuff and close the seam. Attach the head to the body. Seam and stuff the feet. Attach the arms, feet, ears and tail. Using dark brown DK (8-ply) yarn, embroider each eye with a French knot and embroider the nose and mouth with backstitch.

Starting at the fasten-off end of the acorn, sew the seam leaving a gap for stuffing. Stuff and close the seam. Work a gathering thread along the cast-on edge, pull tightly and fasten off. Create a stalk on the top centre of the shell by backstitching on the same spot, two or three times with dark brown DK (8-ply) yarn. Attach the acorn to the squirrel's arms using light brown yarn.

Beach bunnies

Instructions

Blue bunny

Body

The piece is knitted in striped st/st. Do not break the yarn each time you change colour. Slide the sts to the end of the needle and continue.

Starting with the neck, cast on 10 sts with light blue yarn.
Row 1: p.
Row 2: kf/b in each st (20).
Row 3: p.
Join in blue yarn.
Row 4: k blue. Slide sts to end of needle and continue.
Row 5: k light blue.
Row 6: p light blue. Slide sts to end of needle and continue.
Row 7: p blue.
Row 8: k light blue.
Row 9: p light blue.
Row 10: k blue. Slide sts to end of needle and continue.
Row 11: k light blue.
Row 12: (p1, p2tog, p1) to end with light blue (15). Slide sts to end of needle and continue.
Row 13: p blue.
Row 14: k light blue.
Row 15: p light blue.
Break yarn, draw through sts, pull tightly and fasten off.

Head

Starting with the back of the head, cast on 9 sts with white yarn.
Row 1: p.
Row 2: kf/b in each st (18).
Rows 3–8: st/st.
Row 9: (p2tog, p1) to end (12).
Break yarn, draw through sts, pull tightly and fasten off.

Feet: make two

Starting with the back of the foot, cast on 8 sts with white yarn.
Row 1: p.
Row 2: k.
Row 3: (p1, pf/b) to last 2 sts, p2 (11).
Rows 4–7: st/st.
Row 8: k2, k2tog, k3, k2tog, k2 (9).
Break yarn, draw through sts, pull tightly and fasten off.

Arms: make two

Cast on 6 sts with white yarn and work an i-cord for 5 rows (see page 21). Break yarn, draw through sts, pull tightly and fasten off.

Ears: make two

Cast on 4 sts with white yarn.
Rows 1–4: st/st, starting with a p row.
Row 5: p1, p2tog, p1 (3).
Row 6: skpo, k1 (2).
Pass the first stitch over the second stitch and fasten off.

Float

Cast on 10 sts with white yarn and, starting with a k row, work in striped st/st (4 rows white, 3 rows red) five times.
Cast off.

Materials

- DK (8-ply) yarn: 20g (¾oz), white for both bunnies
- DK (8-ply) yarn: 4g (⅛oz) light blue and light pink
- DK (8-ply) yarn: small amounts of blue, red, pink and yellow
- Fingering (4-ply) yarn: small amount of dark brown or two strands taken from dark brown DK (8-ply) yarn
- Stuffing

Size

Standing: 8cm (3¼in)
Sitting: 7cm (2¾in)

Difficulty level

Intermediate

To make up

Sew the body seam, leaving a gap for stuffing. Stuff and close the seam. Sew the head seam, leaving a gap for stuffing. Stuff and close the seam. Repeat for each foot. Attach the feet to the base of the body. Attach the head, arms and ears. Using dark brown fingering (4-ply) yarn or two strands taken from dark brown DK (8-ply) yarn, embroider each eye with a French knot and a nose and mouth with backstitch (see page 22). Sew the cast-on and cast-off edges of the float together and sew the seam. Place the bunny inside the float and attach his arms to it.

Pink bunny

Body

Follow the instructions given for the blue bunny, using light pink yarn instead of light blue yarn, and pink yarn instead of blue yarn.

Arms, ears and feet

As given for the blue bunny.

Head

As given for the blue bunny, but omit 1 row from st/st rows.

To make up

Follow the instructions given for the blue bunny. Attach the feet on the sides of the body instead of the base of the body.
Omit the float.

Beach ball

Cast on 25 sts with yellow yarn.
Join in light pink yarn and light blue yarn.
Row 1: p5 yellow, p4 light pink, p4 light blue, p4 yellow, 4 light pink, p4 light blue.
Rows 2–11: keeping the colours correct, st/st.
Break off light pink yarn and light blue yarn and continue with yellow yarn.
Row 12: (k2tog) to last st, k1 (13).
Break yarn, draw through sts, pull tightly and fasten off.

To make up

Starting at the fasten-off end of the beach ball, sew the seam and stuff. Work a gathering thread along the cast-on edge, pull tightly and fasten off to shape the ball.

Fun finger puppets

Materials

Rabbit:

DK (8-ply) yarn: small amounts of pink, white, dark brown and light brown

Cat:

DK (8-ply) yarn: small amounts of light blue, dark grey, white, pink and black

Bear:

DK (8-ply) yarn: small amounts of yellow, brown, beige and dark brown

Dog:

DK (8-ply) yarn: small amounts of green, beige, white, brown and dark brown

Pig:

DK (8-ply) yarn: small amounts of beige, light pink and dark brown

All puppets require a small amount of stuffing

Size

Rabbit: 11cm (4¼in) tall, including ears

Cat: 8.5cm (3³/₈in) tall

Bear: 8.5cm (3³/₈in) tall

Dog: 8cm (3¼in) tall

Pig: 8cm (3¼in) tall

Difficulty level

Beginner

Instructions

Rabbit

Body and head

Cast on 20 sts with pink yarn.
Row 1 (WS): (k1, p1) to end.
Rows 2–3: as row 1.
Rows 4–17: st/st, starting with a k row.
Row 18: (k2tog) to end (10).
Change to white yarn.
Row 19: p.
Row 20: kf/b in each st (20).
Rows 21–30: st/st.
Row 31: (p2tog) to end (10).
Break yarn, draw through sts, pull tightly and fasten off.

Muzzle

Cast on 12 sts with white yarn.
Row 1: (p2, p2tog) to end (9).
Row 2: (k2tog) to last st, k1 (5).
Break yarn, draw through sts, pull tightly and fasten off.

Ears: make two

Cast on 8 sts with white yarn.
Rows 1–4: st/st, starting with a p row.
Row 5: p1, p2tog, p2, p2tog, p1 (6).
Row 6: k.
Row 7: (p2tog) to end (3).
Break yarn, draw through sts, pull tightly and fasten off.

Arms: make two

Cast on 7 sts with white yarn and work an i-cord for 5 rows (see page 21). Break yarn, draw through sts, pull tightly and fasten off.

To make up

Sew the body and head seam. Stuff the head. Work a gathering thread around the neck, pull tightly and fasten off. Starting at the fasten-off end of the muzzle, sew the seam following the instructions given on page 20 and make it into a circle.

Attach the arms, ears and muzzle. Using dark brown DK (8-ply) yarn, embroider each eye with a French knot and a nose and mouth with backstitch. Embroider whiskers with two strands taken from light brown DK (8-ply) yarn.

Cat

Body and head

Follow the instructions given for the rabbit until row 30, using light blue yarn for the body and dark grey yarn for the head. Cast off instead of drawing through sts.

Muzzle

Cast on 18 sts with white yarn.
Row 1: p2, (p2tog, p2) to end (14).
Row 2: (k2tog) to end (7).
Break yarn, draw through sts, pull tightly and fasten off.

Arms: make two

Cast on 7 sts with light blue yarn.
Rows 1–2: st/st, starting with a p row.
Row 3: k.
With the right side facing, join dark grey yarn.
Rows 4–5: st/st, starting with a k row.
Break yarn, draw through sts, pull tightly and fasten off.

To make up

Sew the body and head seam. Stuff the head. Work a gathering thread around the neck, pull tightly and fasten off. With the body and head seam at the centre of the back, sew across the cast-off sts, to form the top of the head. Sew through both layers of the top corners of the head to create triangular ears. Embroider the centre of the ears with white DK (8-ply) yarn and backstitch. Seam the arms without stuffing, and attach them. Starting at the fasten-off end of the muzzle, sew the seam. Attach the muzzle to the face, leaving a small opening for stuffing. Stuff and finish sewing. Using black DK (8-ply) yarn, embroider each eye with a French knot and a nose with backstitch. Using two strands taken from pink DK (8-ply) yarn, embroider three whiskers on either side of the nose.

Bear

Body and head

Follow the instructions given for the rabbit, using yellow yarn for the body and brown yarn for the head.

Arms: make two

Follow the instructions given for the rabbit, using brown yarn.

Muzzle

Follow the instructions given for the cat, using beige yarn.

Ears: make two

Cast on 8 sts with brown yarn. Break yarn, draw through sts, pull tightly and fasten off.

To make up

Follow the instructions given for the rabbit, omitting the whiskers.

Dog

Body and head

Follow the instructions given for the rabbit, using green yarn for the body and beige yarn for the head.

Arms: make two

Follow the instructions given for the cat, using green yarn and beige yarn.

Muzzle

Follow the instructions given for the cat, using white yarn.

Ears: make two

Cast on 8 sts with brown yarn.
Row 1: p.
Row 2: k1, k2tog, k2, k2tog, k1 (6).
Break yarn, draw through sts, pull tightly and fasten off.

To make up

Follow the instructions given for the rabbit, omitting the whiskers.

Pig

Body and head

Follow the instructions given for the rabbit, using beige yarn for the body and light pink yarn for the head.

Arms: make two

Follow the instructions given for the rabbit, using light pink yarn.

Ears: make two

Cast on 5 sts with light pink yarn.
Row 1: p.
Row 2: k2tog, k1, k2tog (3).
Row 3: p2tog, p1 (2).
Row 4: k2tog and fasten off.

Snout

Cast on 10 sts with light pink yarn. Break yarn, draw through sts, pull tightly and fasten off.

To make up

Follow the instructions given for the rabbit, omitting the muzzle, whiskers, nose and mouth.
Using the fasten-off end, stitch up the snout and make it into a small bobble. Attach the snout and embroider nostrils in backstitch with two strands taken from dark brown DK (8-ply) yarn.

Deadly dinosaurs

Stegosaurus

Instructions

Body, head, legs and tail

Cast on 4 sts with light green yarn.
Row 1: k1, (kf/b) twice, k1 (6).
Row 2: p.
Row 3: k2, (kf/b) twice, k2 (8).
Row 4: p.
Row 5: k3, (kf/b) twice, k3 (10).
Row 6: p.
Row 7: k4, (kf/b) twice, k4 (12).
Row 8: p.
Row 9: k5, (kf/b) twice, k5 (14).
Row 10: p.
Row 11: cast on 3 sts, k these sts, k6, (kf/b) twice, k6 (19).
Row 12: cast on 3 sts, p to end (22).
Row 13: k9, (kf/b) four times, k9 (26).
Row 14: p.
Row 15: k11, (kf/b) four times, k11 (30).
Row 16: p.
Row 17: cast off 3 sts, k7, (kf/b) four times, k to end (31).
Row 18: cast off 3 sts, p to end (28).
Row 19: k12, (kf/b) four times, k12 (32).
Row 20: p.
Row 21: cast on 3 sts, k to end (35).
Row 22: cast on 3 sts, p to end (38).
Row 23: k.
Row 24: p.
Row 25: k15, (k2tog) four times, k15 (34).
Row 26: p.
Row 27: cast off 3 sts, k9, (k2tog) four times, k to end (27).
Row 28: cast off 3 sts, p to end (24).
Row 29: cast off 2 sts, k to end (22).
Row 30: cast off 2 sts, p4, p2tog, p5, p2tog, p to end (18).
Rows 31–35: st/st.
Row 36: (p1, p2tog) to end (12).
Row 37: (k2tog) to end (6).
Break yarn, draw through sts, pull tightly and fasten off.

Under-body

Cast on 10 sts with light green yarn.
Rows 1–5: st/st, starting with a k row.
Row 6: cast off 3 sts, p to end (7).
Row 7: cast off 3 sts, k to end (4).
Row 8: p.
Row 9: k.
Row 10: cast on 3 sts, p to end (7).
Row 11: cast on 3 sts, k to end (10).
Rows 12–16: st/st.
Cast off.

Large back spikes: make three

The spikes are worked in g-st.
Cast on 4 sts with dark green yarn.
Row 1: k.
Row 2: k1, (kf/b) twice, k1 (6).
Rows 3–5: k1, skpo, k to end (3).
Row 6: k1, skpo (2).
Row 7: k2tog and fasten off.

Materials
Stegosaurus:

DK (8-ply) yarn: 8g (1/3oz), light green

DK (8-ply) yarn: small amounts of dark green, dark brown and yellow

Stuffing

Size
10cm (4in) long, 6cm (2½in) tall

Difficulty level
Beginner

Small back spikes: make two

The spikes are worked in g-st.
Cast on 3 sts with dark green yarn.
Row 1: k1, kf/b/f, k1 (5).
Rows 2–3: k1, skpo, k to end (3).
Row 4: k1, skpo (2).
Row 5: k2tog and fasten off.

To make up

Sew the head from the fasten-off end, stopping at the front legs. Sew the tail from the cast-on end, stopping at the back legs. Attach the under-body, leaving a gap for stuffing; when you sew the under-body piece to the body, the legs are created. Stuff and close the seam. Attach the spikes on the back – see the picture for guidance. Using two strands taken from dark brown DK (8-ply) yarn, embroider each eye with a French knot, and the nose and mouth with backstitch. With yellow DK (8-ply) yarn, embroider French knots on the dinosaur's back.

Diplodocus

Body, head, legs and tail

Cast on 4 sts with grey-green yarn and follow the instructions given for the stegosaurus (page 64) to the end of row 30.

Row 31: k.
Row 32: p.
Row 33: k5, yb, sl1, yf, turn, sl1, p to end.
Row 34: k6, yb, sl1, yf, turn, sl1, p to end.
Row 35: k to end.
Row 36: p5, yb, sl1, yf, turn, sl1, k to end.
Row 37: p6, yb, sl1, yf, turn, sl1, k to end.
Row 38: p across all sts.
Row 39–44: st/st.
Row 45: k2, (k2tog, k2) to end (14).
Rows 46–54: st/st.
Row 55: cast on 3 sts, k to end (17).
Row 56: cast on 3 sts, p to end (20).
Rows 57–59: st/st.
Row 60: p2tog, p to last 2 sts, p2tog (18).
Cast off.

Under-body

Cast on 10 sts with grey-green yarn.
Rows 1–5: st/st, starting with a k row.

Row 6: cast off 3 sts, p to end (7).
Row 7: cast off 3 sts, k to end (4).
Row 8: p.
Row 9: k.
Row 10: cast on 3 sts, p to end (7).
Row 11: cast on 3 sts, k to end (10).
Rows 12–16: st/st.
Cast off.

To make up

Sew the neck and head seam, folding the piece vertically and stuff. Make up the body and tail as for the stegosaurus (page 64). Attach the under-body, leaving a gap for stuffing; when you attach the under-body, the legs are created. Stuff and close the seam. Secure the base of the neck to the body to keep the head upright. See the picture for guidance. With yellow yarn, embroider the spots with short backstitch. With dark brown DK (8-ply) yarn, embroider each eye with a French knot and the nose and mouth with backstitch (see page 22).

Materials

Diplodocus:

DK (8-ply) yarn: 10g (1/3oz), grey-green

DK (8-ply) yarn: small amounts of yellow and dark brown

Stuffing

Triceratops:

DK (8-ply) yarn: 8g (1/3oz), red-brown

DK (8-ply) yarn: small amounts of white, dark brown, light orange

Stuffing

Size

Diplodocus: 9cm (3½in) long, 9cm (3½in) tall

Triceratops: 10cm (4in) long, 6cm (2½in) tall

Difficulty level

Beginner

Triceratops

Body, head, legs and tail

Cast on 4 sts with red-brown yarn and follow the instructions given for the stegosaurus (page 64) to the end of row 14.

Row 15: k12, (kf/b) twice, k12 (28).
Row 16: p.
Row 17: cast off 3 sts, k9, (kf/b) twice, k to end (27).
Row 18: cast off 3 sts, p to end (24).
Row 19: k.
Row 20: p.
Row 21: cast on 3 sts, k to end (27).
Row 22: cast on 3 sts, p to end (30).
Row 23: k.
Row 24: p.
Row 25: k13, (k2tog) twice, k to end (28).
Row 26: p.
Row 27: cast off 3 sts, k8, (k2tog) twice, k to end (23).
Row 28: cast off 3 sts, p to end (20).
Row 29: cast off 3 sts, k to end (17).
Row 30: cast off 3 sts, p to end (14).
Rows 31–34: st/st.
Row 35: (k1, k2tog) to last 2 sts, k2 (10).
Rows 36–38: st/st.
Row 39: (k2tog) to end (5).
Break yarn, draw through sts, pull tightly and fasten off.

Under-body

Cast on 10 sts with red-brown yarn.
Rows 1–5: st/st, starting with a k row.
Row 6: cast off 3 sts, p to end (7).
Row 7: cast off 3 sts, k to end (4).
Row 8: p.
Row 9: k.
Row 10: cast on 3 sts, p to end (7).
Row 11: cast on 3 sts, k to end (10).
Rows 12–16: st/st.
Cast off.

Neck piece

Cast on 10 sts with red-brown yarn.
Row 1: (kf/b, k1) to end (15).
Row 2: k.
Row 3: (k2, kf/b) to end (20).
Row 4: k.
Row 5: (k3, kf/b) to end (25).
Row 6: k.
Break yarn, leaving a long end.
To finish off the neck piece, thread red-brown yarn through a sewing needle. Transfer the first 2 sts onto the sewing needle, removing them from your knitting needle. Pull the thread through the 2 sts. Insert the sewing needle back through the same 2 sts and pull through again (see diagram below). Then, take the next 2 sts on the knitting needle and repeat this process across the row.

Large horns: make two

Cast on 3 sts with white yarn and work an i-cord for 5 rows (see page 21).
Next row: k2tog, k1 (2).
Pass the first stitch over the second stitch and fasten off.

Small horn: make one

Cast on 3 sts with white yarn.
Next row: p2tog, p1 (2).
Pass the first stitch over the second stitch and fasten off.

To make up

Make up the body, head, legs and tail as for the stegosaurus (page 64); when you attach the under-body, the legs are created. Attach the neck piece to the body. Attach the horns. With dark brown DK (8-ply) yarn, embroider each eye with a French knot and the nose and mouth with backstitch (see page 22). With light orange yarn, embroider the back with long backstitches.

Plesiosaurus

Body, head, legs and tail

Cast on 4 sts with light blue yarn.
Row 1: k1, (kf/b) twice, k1 (6).
Row 2: p.
Row 3: k2, (kf/b) twice, k2 (8).
Row 4: p.
Row 5: k3, (kf/b) twice, k3 (10).
Row 6: p.
Row 7: k4, (kf/b) twice, k4 (12).
Row 8: p.
Row 9: k5, (kf/b) twice, k5 (14).
Row 10: p.
Row 11: cast on 5 sts, k these sts, k6, (kf/b) twice, k to end (21).
Row 12: cast on 5 sts, p to end (26).
Row 13: skpo, k9, (kf/b) four times, k to last 2 sts, k2tog (28).
Row 14: p.
Row 15: skpo, k10, (kf/b) four times, k to last 2 sts, k2tog (30).
Row 16: p.
Row 17: cast off 2 sts, k10, (kf/b) four times, k to end (32).
Row 18: cast off 2 sts, p to end (30).
Row 19: k13, (kf/b) four times, k to end (34).
Row 20: p.
Row 21: cast on 5 sts, k to end (39).
Row 22: cast on 5 sts, p to end (44).
Row 23: skpo, k to last 2 sts, k2tog (42).
Row 24: p.
Row 25: skpo, k15, (k2tog) four times, k to last 2 sts, k2tog (36).
Row 26: p.
Row 27: cast off 2 sts, k11, (k2tog) four times, k to end (30).
Row 28: cast off 2 sts, p to end (28).
Row 29: k5, yf, sl1, yb, turn, sl1, p to end.
Row 30: k6, yf, sl1, yb, turn, sl1, p to end.
Row 31: k across all sts.
Row 32: p5, yb, sl1, yf, turn, sl1, k to end.
Row 33: p6, yb, sl1, yf, turn, sl1, k to end.
Row 34: p across all sts.
Row 35: (k2, k2tog) to end (21).
Rows 36–40: st/st.
Row 41: (k2, k2tog) to last st, k1 (16).
Row 42: p.
Row 43: k2tog, k to last 2 sts, k2tog (14).
Rows 44–48: st/st.
Row 49: cast on 3 sts, k to end (17).
Row 50: cast on 3 sts, p to end (20).
Rows 51–53: st/st.
Cast off.

Under-body

Cast on 15 sts with light blue yarn.
Row 1: p.
Row 2: skpo, k to last 2 sts, k2tog (13).
Row 3: p.
Row 4: as row 2 (11).
Row 5: p.
Row 6: as row 2 (9).
Rows 7–9: st/st.
Row 10: cast on 5 sts, k to end (14).
Row 11: cast on 5 sts, p to end (19).
Row 12: skpo, k to last 2 sts, k2tog (17).
Row 13: p.
Row 14: as row 12 (15).
Row 15: p.
Row 16: as row 12 (13).
Row 17: p.
Row 18: as row 12 (11).
Row 19: p.
Row 20: as row 12 (9).
Cast off.

To make up

Make up the body, head, legs and tail as for the stegosaurus (page 64); when you attach the under-body, the legs are created. With purple yarn, embroider the spots with short backstitch. With dark brown DK (8-ply) yarn, embroider each eye with a French knot and the nose and mouth with backstitch (see page 22).

Materials

Plesiosaurus:

DK (8-ply) yarn: 15g (½oz), light blue

DK (8-ply) yarn: small amounts of purple and dark brown

Stuffing

Pterodactyl:

DK (8-ply) yarn: 10g (⅓oz), light orange

DK (8-ply) yarn: small amounts of red-brown and dark brown

Stuffing

Additional equipment

Spare needle or stitch holder

Size

Plesiosaurus: 8cm (3¼in) long, 9cm (3½in) tall

Pterodactyl: 7cm (2¾in) long, 11cm (4¼in) wide wing span

Difficulty level

Beginner

Pterodactyl

Body and legs

* Cast on 6 sts with light orange yarn and st/st 4 rows, starting with a k row.

Break off the yarn and keep the sts on a stitch holder. Repeat from * but do not break off the yarn.

With right side facing, place the first piece on the left side of this piece on the same needle and continue.

Row 5: (k1, kf/b) to end, across both pieces to connect (18).

Row 6: p.

Row 7: k12, yb, sl1, yf, turn.

Rows 8–14: st/st.

Row 15: k2, (k2tog, k2) to end (14).

Row 16: p.

Row 17: (k2tog) to end (7).

Rows 18–19: st/st.

Break yarn, draw through sts, pull tightly and fasten off.

Head

Cast on 5 sts with light orange yarn.

Row 1: p.

Row 2: kf/b in each st (10).

Row 3: p.

Rows 4–7: st/st.

Row 8: (k2, kf/b) to last st, k1 (13).

Rows 9–10: st/st.

Row 11: (p2tog) to last st, p1 (7).

Break yarn, draw through sts, pull tightly and fasten off.

Wings: make two

Cast on 15 sts with light orange yarn.

Row 1: p7, k1, p7.

Row 2: k.

Row 3: as row 1.

Row 4: k.

Row 5: p.

Row 6: skpo, k to last 2 sts, k2tog (13).

Row 7: p6, k1, p6.

Row 8: k.

Row 9: as row 7.

Row 10: k.

Row 11: as row 7.

Row 12: skpo, k to last 2 sts, k2tog (11).

Row 13: p5, k1, p5.

Row 14: k.

Row 15: as row 13.

Row 16: skpo, k to last 2 sts, k2tog (9).

Row 17: p4, k1, p4.

Row 18: skpo, k to last 2 sts, k2tog (7).

Row 19: p3, k1, p3.

Row 20: skpo, k to last 2 sts, k2tog (5).

Row 21: p2tog, k1, p2tog (3).

Break yarn, draw through sts, pull tightly and fasten off.

To make up

Sew the body and legs seam, leaving a gap for stuffing. Stuff lightly and close the seam. Repeat with the head and wings. With the body and legs seam facing down, attach the wings and the head.

Embroider the spots with red-brown yarn and French knots.

With dark brown DK (8-ply) yarn, embroider each eye with a French knot and a mouth with backstitch.

Perfect penguins

Instructions

Body and head

Cast on 7 sts with black yarn.
Row 1: kf/b in each st (14).
Row 2: p.
Row 3: (k1, kf/b) to end (21).
Row 4: k for fold line.
Join in white yarn.
Row 5: k7 black, k7 white,
k7 black.
Row 6: Keeping the colours
correct, p.
Row 7: keeping the colours
correct, k, decrease 1 st at both
ends (19).
Rows 8–13: keeping the colours
correct, st/st, starting with a p row.
Row 14: break off white yarn and
continue with black yarn only, p.
Row 15: k1, (k2tog, k1) to end
(13).
Rows 16–19: st/st.
Row 20: (p2, p2tog) to last st,
p1 (10).
Break yarn, draw through sts, pull
tightly and fasten off.

Wings: make two

Cast on 10 sts with black yarn.
Rows 1–3: st/st, starting with a
p row.
Row 4: k1, (k2tog, k1) to end (7).
Rows 5–7: st/st.
Row 8: (k2tog) to last st, k1 (4).
Break yarn, draw through sts, pull
tightly and fasten off.

Feet: make two

The feet are worked in garter stitch.
Cast on 4 sts with orange yarn.
Rows 1–3: k.
Row 4: k1, k2tog, k1 (3).
Rows 5–6: k.
Cast off.

Beak

Cast on 7 sts with orange yarn.
Row 1: p2tog, p3, p2tog (5).
Row 2: skpo, k1, k2tog (3).
Row 3: p2tog, p1 (2).
Pass the first stitch over the
second stitch and fasten off.

Scarf

Cast on 3 sts with fine kid mohair
yarn or fingering (4-ply) yarn in
your choice of colour. Work an
i-cord for 12cm (4¾in) (see page
21). Cast off.
Make small tassels with backstitch
and matching yarn, leaving a loop
every other stitch. Cut the loops to
make the tassels.

To make up

Starting at the fasten-off end,
sew the body and head seam,
leaving a gap for stuffing. Work a
gathering thread along the cast-on
edge, pull tightly and fasten. Stuff
the body and head and close the
seam. Fold each wing vertically
and attach to the body. Attach
the beak. Using two strands
taken from white DK (8-ply) yarn,
embroider each eye with tiny
backstitches. Attach the feet
and the scarf.

Materials

DK (8-ply) yarn: 3g (¹/₁₀oz),
  black

DK (8-ply) yarn: small
  amounts of white
  and orange

Fine kid mohair or fingering
  (4-ply) yarn: small amount
  of your choice of colour for
  the scarf

Stuffing

Size

4cm (1½in) tall

Difficulty level

Beginner

Alien invasion!

Instructions

UFO

Top

Cast on 13 sts with red yarn.
Row 1: p.
Row 2: kf/b in each st (26).
Row 3: p.
Row 4: (k1, kf/b) to end (39).
Row 5: p.
Row 6: (k2, kf/b) to end (52).
Rows 7–8: st/st.
Row 9: k for edge.
Row 10: k.
Divide stitches equally on to 3 double-pointed knitting needles and continue working in rounds.
Rnds 1–10: k.
Rnd 11: (k2, k2tog) to end (39).
Rnds 12–14: k.
Change to orange yarn.
Rnds 15–16: k.
Change to grey yarn.
Rnds 17–18: k.
Rnd 19: (k2tog) to last st, k1 (20).
Rnds 20–21: k.
Row 22: (k2tog) to end (10).
Break yarn, draw through sts, pull tightly and fasten off.

Disk

Cast on 7 sts with grey yarn.
Row 1: p.
Row 2: kf/b in each st (14).
Row 3: p.
Row 4: (k1, kf/b) to end (21).
Row 5: p.
Row 6: (k2, kf/b) to end (28).

Row 7: p.
Row 8: (k3, kf/b) to end (35).
Row 9: p.
Row 10: (k4, kf/b) to end (42).
Row 11: p.
Row 12: (k5, kf/b) to end (49).
Row 13: p.
Row 14: (k6, kf/b) to end (56).
Row 15: p.
Row 16: (k7, kf/b) to end (63).
Row 17: p.
Change to red yarn.
Row 18: (k8, kf/b) to end (70).
Row 19: p.
Row 20: (k9, kf/b) to end (77).
Row 21: k for fold line.
Row 22: (k9, k2tog) to end (70).
Row 23: p.
Change to orange yarn.
Row 24: (k8, k2tog) to end (63).
Row 25: p.
Change to grey yarn.
Row 26: (k7, k2tog) to end (56).
Work the rest with grey.
Row 27: p.
Row 28: (k6, k2tog) to end (49).
Row 29: p.
Row 30: (k5, k2tog) to end (42).
Row 31: p.
Row 32: (k4, k2tog) to end (35).
Row 33: p.
Row 34: (k3, k2tog) to end (28).
Row 35: p.
Row 36: (k2, k2tog) to end (21).
Row 37: p.
Row 38: (k1, k2tog) to end (14).
Row 39: p.
Row 40: (k2tog) to end (7).
Break yarn, draw through sts, pull tightly and fasten off.

continued overleaf

Materials

UFO:

DK (8-ply) yarn: 15g (½oz), grey

DK (8-ply) yarn: 10g (⅓oz), red

DK (8-ply) yarn: 10g (⅓oz), yellow

DK (8-ply) yarn: small amounts of orange, white and blue

Lightweight cardboard circle, 10cm (4in) in diameter

Stuffing

Aliens:

DK (8-ply) yarn: small amounts of yellow, light green, light blue, purple, blue-green and mid-blue

Fingering (4-ply) yarn: small amounts of dark grey and white or two strands taken from dark grey and white DK (8-ply) yarn

Additional equipment

You will need four double-pointed needles

Size

UFO: 10cm (4in) in diameter, 8cm (3¼in) tall

Aliens: 3cm (1¼in) tall

Difficulty level

Intermediate

Yellow domes under the disk: make four

Cast on 7 sts with yellow yarn.
Row 1: p.
Row 2: kf/b in each st (14).
Row 3: p.
Row 4: (k1, kf/b) to end (21).
Row 5: k for edge.
Rows 6–11: st/st, starting with a k row.
Row 12: (k1, k2tog) to end (14).
Row 13: p.
Row 14: (k2tog) to end (7).
Break yarn, draw through sts, pull tightly and fasten off.

Windows: make six

Cast on 13 sts with white yarn. Break off white yarn and change to blue yarn.
St/st 2 rows, starting with a k row. Break yarn, draw through sts, pull tightly and fasten off.

Antenna

Cast on 3 sts with grey yarn and work an i-cord for 7 rows (see page 21). Break yarn, draw through sts, pull tightly and fasten off.
For the light, cast on 10 sts with yellow yarn. Break yarn, draw through sts and pull tightly. Attach it to the end of the antenna.

To make up

Sew the seam of the top piece, halfway along. Work a gathering thread along the cast-on edge, pull tightly and fasten off. Stuff and close the seam.

For the disk, work a gathering thread along the cast-on edge, pull tightly and fasten off. Sew the seam of the disk, halfway along. Insert the cardboard circle and close the seam. Attach the disk to the top piece, using the picture for guidance. Make up the yellow domes in the same way as the top piece and attach them under the disk. Sew the seam of each window and attach around the top piece. Attach the antenna to the top.

Yellow alien

Body and head

Cast on 5 sts with yellow yarn.
Row 1: p.
Row 2: kf/b in each st (10).
Row 3: k for edge.
Rows 4–7: st/st, starting with a k row.
Row 8: (k2tog) to end (5).
Row 9: p.
Row 10: kf/b in each st (10).
Row 11: p.
Row 12: k.
Row 13: (p2, pf/b) to last st, p1 (13).
Row 14: k.
Row 15: p.
Row 16: (k2tog) to last st, k1 (7).
Break yarn, draw through sts, pull tightly and fasten off.

Feet: make two

Cast on 3 sts with yellow yarn and st/st 7 rows, starting with a k row. Cast off.

Eyes: make two

Cast on 8 sts with dark grey fingering (4-ply) yarn or two strands taken from dark grey DK (8-ply) yarn. Break off yarn, draw through sts, pull tightly and fasten off.

To make up

Make up the body and head and flatten the base following the instructions on pages 16–18. Make up the eyes following the instructions on page 20 and sew them to the body, stretching one end to make a slightly oval shape. Attach the feet to the base of the body. See the picture for guidance.

Googly-eyed alien

Body

Cast on 4 sts with light green yarn.
Row 1: kf/b in each st (8).
Row 2: k for the edge.
Row 3: (k1, kf/b) to end (12).
Row 4: p.
Row 5: (k1, kf/b) to end (18).
Rows 6–10: st/st.
Row 11: (k1, k2tog) to end (12).
Row 12: p.
Break yarn, draw through sts, pull tightly and fasten off.

Eyes: make two

Cast on 10 sts with white fingering (4-ply) yarn or two strands taken from white DK (8-ply) yarn. Break yarn, draw through sts, pull tightly and fasten off.

Antennae: make two

For the first antenna, cast on 2 sts with light green yarn and work an i-cord for 3 rows (see page 21).
For the second antenna, cast on 2 sts with light green yarn and work an i-cord for 6 rows.

Feet: make two

Cast on 3 sts with light green yarn and st/st 7 rows, starting with a k row. Cast off.

To make up

Make up the body and head and flatten the base following the instructions on pages 16–18. Make up the eyes following the instructions on page 20 and sew to the antennae. Using dark grey fingering (4-ply) yarn or two strands taken from dark grey DK (8-ply), embroider the centre of each eye with a French knot and the mouth with backstitch. Hide the yarn ends inside the antennae and attach the antennae to the body. Attach the feet to the base of the body. See the picture for guidance.

Three-eyed alien

Body

The body is knitted in striped st/st. Do not break the yarn each time you change colour. Slide the sts to the end of the needle and continue.

Cast on 6 sts with light blue yarn.

Row 1: p.

Row 2: kf/b in each st (12).

Row 3: p.

Row 4: (k1, kf/b) to end (18).

Row 5: p.

Row 6: k.

Join in purple yarn, do not break off light blue yarn.

Row 7: p. Slide sts to end of needle and continue.

Row 8: p with light blue yarn.

Row 9: k with light blue yarn. Slide sts to end of needle and continue.

Row 10: k with purple yarn.

Break off purple yarn and continue with light blue yarn.

Rows 11–15: st/st, starting with a p row.

Row 16: (k2tog) to end (9).

Break yarn, draw through sts, pull tightly and fasten off.

Arms: make two

Cast on 2 sts with purple yarn and work an i-cord for 3 rows (see page 21). Pass the first stitch over the second stitch and fasten off.

Eyes: make three

Cast on 6 sts with white fingering (4-ply) yarn or two strands taken from white DK (8-ply) yarn. Break yarn, draw through sts, pull tightly and fasten off.

Antenna

Cast on 2 sts with purple yarn and work an i-cord for 3 rows.

Pass the first stitch over the second stitch and fasten off.

Top of the antenna

Cast on 6 sts with purple yarn. Break yarn, draw through sts, pull tightly and fasten off.

To make up

Make up the body and head and flatten the base following the instructions on pages 16–18. Make up the eyes following the instructions on page 20 and attach them to the body. Using dark grey fingering (4-ply) yarn or two strands taken from dark grey DK (8-ply), embroider the centre of each eye with a French knot. Attach the arms and the antenna. Attach the top of the antenna.

One-eyed alien

Body

Cast on 5 sts with blue-green yarn.

Row 1: p.

Row 2: kf/b in each st (10).

Row 3: p.

Row 4: (k1, kf/b) to end (15).

Row 5: k for the edge.

Rows 6–7: st/st, starting with a k row.

Row 8: (k2, k2tog) to last 3 sts, k3 (12).

Rows 9–14: st/st.

Row 15: (p1, p2tog) to end (8).

Break yarn, draw through sts, pull tightly and fasten off.

Outer eye piece

Cast on 12 sts with white yarn. Break yarn, draw through sts, pull tightly and fasten off.

Inner eye piece

Cast on 6 sts with light blue yarn. Break yarn, draw through sts, pull tightly and fasten off.

Antennae: make two

Cast on 2 sts with blue-green yarn and work an i-cord for 3 rows. Without breaking off the yarn, cast on 6 sts. Break yarn, draw through sts, pull tightly and fasten off.

To make up

Make up the body and flatten the base following the instructions on pages 16–18. Make up the eye pieces following the instructions on page 20 and sew to the body. Using dark grey fingering (4-ply) yarn or two strands taken from dark grey DK (8-ply), embroider the centre of the eye with a French knot and the mouth with backstitch. Hide the yarn ends inside each antenna and attach the antennae to the body.

Alien with horn

Body and head

Cast on 5 sts with mid-blue yarn.
Row 1: p.
Row 2: kf/b in each st (10).
Row 3: k for the edge.
Rows 4–8: st/st, starting with a k row.
Row 9: (p2tog) to end (5).
Row 10: kf/b in each st (10).
Row 11: p.
Row 12: (k1, kf/b) to end (15).
Rows 13–17: st/st.
Row 18: (k1, k2tog) to end (10).
Break yarn, draw through sts, pull tightly and fasten off.

Horn

Cast on 3 sts with mid-blue yarn.
Next row: sl1, p2tog (2).
Pass the first stitch over the second stitch and fasten off.

Legs: make two

Cast on 3 sts with mid-blue yarn and st/st 4 rows, starting with a k row. Cast off.

Eyes: make two

Cast on 8 sts with white fingering (4-ply) yarn or two strands taken from white DK (8-ply) yarn. Break yarn, draw through sts, pull tightly and fasten off.

To make up

Make up the body and head and flatten the base following the instructions on pages 16–18. Make up the eyes following the instructions on page 20 and attach them to the head. Using dark grey fingering (4-ply) yarn or two strands taken from dark grey DK (8-ply), embroider the centre of each eye with a French knot. Using mid-blue yarn, create a nose by backstitching on the same spot three times. Attach the legs and the horn.

Mousey mates

Instructions

Big mouse

Body

Starting with the base, cast on 10 sts with cream yarn.
Row 1: p.
Row 2: kf/b in each st (20).
Rows 3–11: st/st.
Row 12: (k1, k2tog, k1) to end (15).
Rows 13–15: st/st.
Break yarn, draw through sts, pull tightly and fasten off.

Head

Starting with the back of the head, cast on 9 sts with cream yarn.
Row 1: p.
Row 2: kf/b in each st (18).
Rows 3–8: st/st.
Row 9: (p1, p2tog) to end (12).
Break yarn, draw through sts, pull tightly and fasten off.

Feet: make two

Starting with the back of the foot, cast on 8 sts with dark brown yarn.
Row 1: p.
Row 2: k.
Row 3: (p1, pf/b) to last 2 sts, p2 (11).
Rows 4–7: st/st.
Row 8: k2, k2tog, k3, k2tog, k2 (9).
Break yarn, draw through sts, pull tightly and fasten off.

Arms: make two

Cast on 6 sts with light green yarn and work an i-cord for 5 rows.

Join in cream yarn and work an i-cord for one more row.
Break yarn, draw through sts, pull tightly and fasten off.

Ears: make two

Cast on 6 sts with cream yarn.
Next row: p1, p2tog, p2tog, p1 (4).
Break yarn, draw through sts, pull tightly and fasten off.

Tail

Cast on 2 sts with cream yarn and work an i-cord for 8 rows.
Pass the first stitch over the second stitch and fasten off.

Coat

Cast on 24 sts with light green yarn and st/st 12 rows, starting with a k row.
Next row: (k2tog) to end (12).
Break yarn, draw through sts, pull tightly and fasten off.

Scarf

Cast on 3 sts with orange yarn and work an i-cord for 7cm (2¾in).
Cast off.

To make up

Sew the body, head and feet seams, leaving a gap for stuffing. Stuff and close the seams. Attach the head, feet and arms to the body. Attach the ears to the head. Sew the fasten-off end of the coat to the neck with the edges meeting in the centre of the front. Using dark brown DK (8-ply) yarn, embroider French knots for buttons, if desired (see page 22). Attach the scarf around the neck. Using dark brown DK (8-ply) yarn, embroider each eye with a French knot and a nose and mouth with backstitch. Embroider whiskers with two strands taken from light brown DK (8-ply) yarn and backstitch. Attach the tail.

Little mouse

Body

Starting with the base, cast on 9 sts with cream yarn.
Row 1: p.
Row 2: kf/b in each st (18).
Rows 3–9: st/st.
Row 10: (k1, k2tog, k1) to last 2 sts, k2 (14).
Rows 11–13: st/st.
Break yarn, draw through sts, pull tightly and fasten off.

Head

Starting with the back of the head, cast on 7 sts with cream yarn.

Row 1: p.

Row 2: kf/b in each st (14).

Rows 3–8: st/st.

Row 9: p2, (p1, p2tog) to end (10). Break yarn, draw through sts, pull tightly and fasten off.

Feet: make two

Starting with the back of the foot, cast on 7 sts with dark brown yarn.

Row 1: p.

Row 2: k.

Row 3: (p1, pf/b) to last st, p1 (10).

Rows 4–7: st/st.

Row 8: k2, (k2tog, k2) twice (8). Break yarn, draw through sts, pull tightly and fasten off.

Coat

Cast on 20 sts with blue yarn and st/st 10 rows, starting with a k row.

Next row: (k2tog) to end (10). Break yarn, draw through sts, pull tightly and fasten off.

Arms: make two

Cast on 6 sts with blue yarn and work an i-cord for 4 rows.

Join in cream yarn and work an i-cord for one more row. Break yarn, draw through sts, pull tightly and fasten off.

Ears and tail

As given for the big mouse.

Scarf

Cast on 3 sts with red yarn and work an i-cord for 6cm (2¼in). Cast off.

To make up

Follow the instructions given for the big mouse.

Pretty parrot

Instructions

Body and head

Starting with the base, cast on 6 sts with light green yarn.
Row 1: p.
Row 2: kf/b to end (12).
Row 3: p.
Row 4: (k2, kf/b) to end (16).
Rows 5–9: st/st.
Row 10: (k1, kf/b) to end (24).
Rows 11–15: st/st.
Row 16: (k1, k2tog) to end (16).
Change to light yellow yarn.
Row 17: p.
Row 18: k4, (kf/b) eight times, turn, p16, turn, sl1, k to end (24).
Rows 19–21: st/st.
Row 22: k4, (k2tog, k1) five times, k2tog, k3 (18).
Rows 23–27: st/st.
Row 28: k2, (k2tog, k2) to end (14).
Break yarn, draw through sts, pull tightly and fasten off.

Wings: make two

Cast on 10 sts with light yellow yarn.
Rows 1–4: st/st, starting with a p row.
Row 5: p1, (p2tog, p1) to end (7).
Row 6: k.
Row 7: (p2tog) three times, p1 (4).
Break yarn, draw through sts, pull tightly and fasten off.

Beak

Cast on 3 sts with orange yarn.
Rows 1–2: st/st, starting with a k row.
Row 3: skpo, k1 (2).
Row 4: p2tog and fasten off.

Tail

Cast on 12 sts with light yellow yarn.
Row 1: (k2, p1) to end.
Row 2: (k1, p2) to end.
Row 3: (k2tog, p1) to end (8).
Rows 4–8: work in k1, p1 rib.
Row 9: (p2tog) to end (4).
Break yarn, draw through sts, pull tightly and fasten off.

Feet: make two

With light pink yarn and a crochet hook, * make 4 chains, miss 2 chains, ss to next 2 chains. Repeat from * three more times.
Fasten off.

Cheek circles: make two

Cast on 8 sts with two strands taken from light blue DK (8-ply) yarn. Break yarn, draw through sts, pull tightly and fasten off.

To make up

Starting at the fasten-off end of the body and head, sew the head seam. Work a gathering thread along the cast-on edge, pull tightly and fasten. Sew the rest of the body seam, leaving a gap for stuffing. Stuff the body, avoiding the neck area and close the seam. Work a gathering thread along the

Materials

DK (8-ply) yarn: small amounts of light green, light yellow, orange, light pink, light blue and dark brown

Stuffing

Additional equipment

3mm (UK 11, US C/2 or D/3) crochet hook

Size

6cm (2¼in) tall

Difficulty level

Beginner

neck and pull tightly to shape. Work a gathering thread on the front of the face to create an eye line (optional). Sew the wing seam without stuffing. Attach wings, feet, tail, cheek circles and the beak. Using dark brown DK (8-ply) yarn, embroider each eye with a French knot. Using dark brown DK (8-ply) yarn, embroider dots on the cheeks with French knots. With light yellow DK (8-ply) yarn, backstitch a few times on top of the head, leaving a loop every other stitch. Cut the loops and separate the strands.

Dressing-up time!

Materials

Bunny baby:

DK (8-ply) yarn: 5g (¹⁄₆oz), light pink

DK (8-ply) yarn: small amounts of skin colour and dark brown

Fingering (4-ply) yarn: small amount of light brown

Chunky, fleecy yarn: small amount of white

Stuffing

Bee baby:

DK (8-ply) yarn: 5g (¹⁄₆oz), yellow

DK (8-ply) yarn: small amounts of dark brown, skin colour, white and brown

Fingering (4-ply) yarn: small amount of light brown

Chunky, fleecy yarn: small amount of white

Stuffing

Bear baby:

DK (8-ply) yarn: 6g (¹⁄₅oz) brown

DK (8-ply) yarn: small amounts of brown and skin colour

Fingering (4-ply) yarn: small amount of light brown

Stuffing

Size
Bunny baby: 7.5cm (3in)

Bee baby: 6cm (2¼in)

Bear baby: 6cm (2¼in)

Difficulty level
Beginner

Instructions

Bunny baby

Body and head

Starting with the base, cast on 7 sts with light pink yarn.
Row 1: p.
Row 2: kf/b in each st (14).
Row 3: p.
Row 4: (k1, kf/b) to end (21).
Rows 5–11: st/st.
Row 12: (k2, k2tog) to last st, k1 (16).
Rows 13–15: st/st.
Row 16: (k2, k2tog) to end (12).
Row 17: change to skin colour yarn and p.
Row 18: k4, (kf/b) four times, k4 (16).
Rows 19–21: st/st.
Row 22: k4, (k2tog, k1) to last 3 sts, k3 (13).
Rows 23–25: st/st.
Row 26: (k2, k2tog) to last st, k1 (10).
Break yarn, draw through sts, pull tightly and fasten off.

Feet: make two

Cast on 5 sts with light pink yarn and work an i-cord for 4 rows. Break yarn, draw through sts, pull tightly and fasten off.

Arms: make two

Cast on 5 sts with light pink yarn and work an i-cord for 5 rows. Change to skin colour yarn and work one row more. Break yarn, draw through sts, pull tightly and fasten off.

Hat

Cast on 24 sts with light pink yarn.
Rows 1–2: st/st, starting with a p row.
Row 3: (p2, p2tog) to end (18).
Row 4: (k2tog) to end (9).
Break yarn, draw through sts, pull tightly and fasten off.

Ears: make two

Cast on 4 sts with light pink yarn.
Rows 1–4: st/st, starting with a k row.
Row 5: k1, k2tog, k1 (3).
Row 6: p2tog, p1 (2).
Row 7: k2tog and fasten off.

To make up

Sew the body and head seam, leaving a gap for stuffing. Stuff, avoiding the neck area, and close the seam. Work a gathering thread around the neck, pull tightly and fasten off.
Flatten the base following the instructions on pages 17–18. Attach the hat, arms, feet and ears. Attach a length of white chunky, fleecy yarn around the neck. Using light brown fingering (4-ply) yarn, backstitch, leaving small loops every stitch to create hair. Use the picture for guidance. Using dark brown DK (8-ply) yarn embroider a French knot for each eye. Create a nose by backstitching several times on the same spot in the centre of the face with skin colour DK (8-ply) yarn.

Bee baby

Body, head, feet, arms and hat

Follow the instructions given for the bunny baby. For the body and head, work rows 1–6 with dark brown yarn, rows 7–8 with yellow yarn, rows 9–10 with dark brown yarn, rows 11–16 with yellow yarn and rows 17–26 with skin colour yarn. Use dark brown for the feet, dark brown and skin colour for the arms and yellow for the hat.

Antennae: make two

Cast on 2 sts with white yarn and work an i-cord for 3 rows (see page 21). Pass the first stitch over the second stitch and fasten off.

To make up

Make up as for the bunny baby, using light brown for the hair.

Bear baby

Body, head, arms, feet and hat

Follow the instructions given for the bunny baby, using brown and skin colour yarn for the body and head and arms and brown for the hat and feet.

Ears: make two

Cast on 8 sts with brown yarn. Break yarn, draw through sts, pull tightly and fasten off.

To make up

Make up as for the bunny baby, omitting the chunky fleecy yarn around the neck.

Cute kangaroos

Instructions

Mummy

Body

Starting with the base, cast on 10 sts with beige yarn.
Row 1: p.
Row 2: kf/b in each st (20).
Rows 3–13: st/st, starting with a p row.
Row 14: (k1, k2tog, k1) to end (15).
Rows 15–19: st/st.
Break yarn, draw through sts, pull tightly and fasten off.

Head

Starting with the back of the head, cast on 8 sts with beige yarn.
Row 1: p.
Row 2: kf/b in each st (16).
Rows 3–9: st/st, starting with a p row.
Row 10: (k1, k2tog, k1) to end (12).
Break yarn, draw through sts, pull tightly and fasten off.

Feet: make two

Starting with the sole of foot, cast on 6 sts with beige yarn.
Row 1: kf/b in each st (12).
Rows 2–4: st/st, starting with a p row.
Row 5: k3, (k3tog) twice, k3 (8).
Rows 6–9: st/st.
Row 10: (p2tog) to end (4).
Break yarn, draw through sts, pull tightly and fasten off.

Tail

Cast on 13 sts with beige yarn.
Rows 1–3: st/st starting with a p row.
Row 4: (k2, k2tog) to last st, k1 (10).
Rows 5–8: st/st.
Row 9: p2, (p2tog, p2) to end (8).
Row 10: k.
Row 11: (p2tog) to end (4).
Row 12: (k2tog) to end (2).
Pass the first stitch over the second stitch and fasten off.

Arms: make two

Cast on 6 sts with beige yarn and work an i-cord for 6 rows (see page 21).
Break yarn, draw through sts, pull tightly and fasten off.

Ears: make two

Cast on 5 sts with beige yarn.
Row 1: p.
Row 2: skpo, k1, k2tog (3).
Break yarn, draw through sts, pull tightly and fasten off.

Dungarees

Cast on 25 sts with red yarn or pink yarn.
Rows 1–12: st/st, starting with a k row.
Row 13: (k1, k2tog, k1) to last st, k1 (19).
Break yarn, draw through sts, pull tightly and fasten off.

Straps: make two

Make 13 chains with red yarn or pink yarn and a crochet hook. Fasten off.

Materials

- DK (8-ply) yarn: 20g (¾oz), beige for both kangaroos
- DK (8-ply) yarn: 4g (⅛oz), red or pink
- Fingering (4-ply) yarn: small amount of dark brown or use two strands taken from dark brown DK (8-ply) yarn
- Stuffing

Additional equipment

3mm (UK 11, US C/2 or D/3) crochet hook

Size

Mummy: 7cm (2¾in) tall

Joey: 3cm (1¼in) tall

Note: the joey is tiny. Sew firmly in place if it is to be given to a small child.

Difficulty level

Beginner

To make up

Sew the body, head, tail and feet seams, leaving a gap for stuffing. Stuff and close the seams. Work a gathering thread around the face to make the eye line (optional). Attach the head to the body. Sew the dungaree seam and attach to the body with the seam at the back. Attach the feet and the tail. Attach the arms and the dungaree straps. Attach the ears to the head. Using dark brown fingering (4-ply) yarn or two strands taken from dark brown DK (8-ply) yarn, embroider each eye with a French knot and a nose and mouth with backstitch.

Joey

Body

Cast on 9 sts with beige yarn.
Rows 1–3: st/st, starting with a
p row.
Row 4: (k2tog, k1) to end (6).
Break yarn, draw through sts, pull
tightly and fasten off.

Head

Cast on 9 sts with beige yarn and
st/st 3 rows starting with a p row.
Break yarn, draw through sts, pull
tightly and fasten off.

Ears: make two

Cast on 2 sts with beige yarn.
Row 1: p.
Pass the first stitch over the
second stitch and fasten off.

Arms: make two

Cast on 2 sts with beige yarn and
work an i-cord for 3 rows. Pass
the first stitch over the second
stitch and fasten off.

To make up

Assemble the joey's body, head,
arms and ears and embroider the
face as for the mummy. Insert the
joey into the mummy's dungarees,
securing firmly with a few stitches if
giving to a small child.

Playful puppies

Instructions

Work the body and legs as one, starting with the hind legs and finishing with the front legs.

Right hind leg

Cast on 7 sts with beige yarn and st/st 6 rows, starting with a k row. Break yarn, and keep the sts on a spare needle or a stitch holder.

Left hind leg

Follow the instructions given for the right hind leg, but do not break off the yarn. With right side facing, place the right hind leg on the left side of the left hind leg on the same needle and continue.
Row 7: k across all sts to connect the two legs (14).
Rows 8–10: st/st, starting with a p row.
Shape the bottom:
Row 11: k9, yf, sl1, yb, turn, sl1, p4, yb, sl1, yf, turn, sl1, k to end (14).
Rows 12–16: st/st.

Front legs

Work the front legs one at a time.
Row 17: k7, turn, p to end.
Row 18: k7, turn, p to end.
Break yarn, draw through sts, pull tightly and fasten off.
With right side facing, rejoin yarn to remaining 7 sts.
Rows 19–22: st/st, starting with a k row.
Break yarn, draw through sts, pull tightly and fasten off.

Head

Starting with the back of the head, cast on 7 sts with beige yarn.
Row 1: k1, (kf/b) to end (13).
Rows 2–6: st/st, starting with a p row.
Row 7: k1, (k2tog, k1) to end (9).
Break yarn, draw through sts, pull tightly and fasten off.

Ears: make two

Cast on 5 sts with brown yarn.
Row 1: p.
Row 2: skpo, k1, k2tog (3).
Break yarn, draw through sts, pull tightly and fasten off.

Tail

Cast on 4 sts with brown yarn.
Row 1: p.
Row 2: k1, skpo, k1 (3).
Row 3: p.
Break yarn, draw through sts, pull tightly and fasten off.

To make up

Sew each leg seam, leaving a small gap in the bottom centre of the body. Stuff the body and close the seam. Sew the seam of the head, leaving a gap for stuffing. Stuff the head and close the seam. Attach the head to the body, with the seam underneath. Attach the ears and tail. Using dark brown fingering (4-ply) yarn or two strands taken from dark brown DK (8-ply) yarn, embroider a French knot for each eye and a nose with backstitch.

Materials

DK (8-ply) yarn:
    15g (½oz), beige

DK (8-ply) yarn: small amount of brown

Fingering (4-ply) yarn: small amount of dark brown yarn or two strands taken from dark brown DK (8-ply) yarn

Stuffing

Additional equipment
Spare needle or stitch holder

Size
5cm (2in) long

Difficulty level
Beginner

Curious cats

Instructions

Cat

Body and legs

Cast on 14 sts with the colour of your choice and st/st 18 rows, starting with a k row. Cast off.

Head

Starting with the back of the head, cast on 14 sts with the colour of your choice.
Rows 1–5: st/st, starting with a p row.
Row 6: (k1, k2tog) to last 2 sts, k2tog (9).
Break yarn, draw through sts, pull tightly and fasten off.

Ears: make two

Cast on 2 sts with the colour of your choice and p 1 row. Pass the first stitch over the second stitch and fasten off.

Tail

Cast on 2 sts with the colour of your choice and work an i-cord for 3cm (1¼in) or desired length. Pass the first stitch over the second stitch and fasten off.

To make up

To create the legs, fold the corners of the body square towards each other and sew them from the tip, using overcast stitch. Stuff the body and sew the seam.
Starting at the fasten-off end of the head, sew the seam and stuff.

Work a gathering thread along the cast-on edge, pull tightly and fasten to close. Hide the fasten-off yarn end of each ear inside the stitches. Attach the head, ears and tail to the body.

Using dark brown fingering (4-ply) yarn or two strands taken from dark brown DK (8-ply) yarn, embroider each eye with a French knot and embroider a nose with backstitch (see page 22). With light brown fingering (4-ply) yarn or two strands taken from light brown DK (8-ply) yarn, embroider the whiskers with backstitch.

Ball of yarn

Thread a 70cm (27½in) length of DK (8-ply) yarn in the colour of your choice on to a sewing needle.
* Roll it from the other, unthreaded end, four or five times, to make a tiny ball and stitch through the ball to secure in place. Repeat from *, several times, until the ball is the right size, leaving a yarn end of your desired length.

Materials

DK (8-ply) yarn: small amount in the colour of your choice

Fingering (4-ply) yarn: small amounts of dark brown and light brown, or two strands taken from dark brown and light brown DK (8-ply) yarn

Stuffing

Size

Cat: 4cm (1½in) long

Ball of yarn: 1cm (½in) in diameter

Difficulty level

Intermediate

Note: you can make the cat in different poses using the same knitting pattern. To make the sleeping cat, sew the legs together at the thighs and attach the head on one side of the body rather than the centre.

Fabulous fairies

Instructions

Body and head

Cast on 6 sts with light blue or pink yarn.
Row 1: p.
Row 2: kf/b in each st (12).
Row 3: p.
Row 4: (k1, kf/b) to end (18).
Rows 5–15: st/st.
Row 16: (k1, k2tog) to end (12).
Change to skin colour yarn.
Row 17: p.
Row 18: k3, (kf/b) six times, k to end (18).
Rows 19–21: st/st.
Row 22: k3, (k1, k2tog) four times, k to end (14).
Rows 23–25: st/st.
Row 26: k2 (k2tog, k2) to end (11).
Break yarn, draw through sts, pull tightly and fasten off.

Skirt

Cast on 36 sts with light blue or pink yarn and st/st four rows, starting with p row.
Next row: (p2tog) to end (18)
Cast off.

Arms: make two

Cast on 4 sts with skin colour yarn and work an i-cord for 6 rows (see page 21). Break yarn, draw through sts, pull tightly and fasten off.

Legs: make two

Cast on 4 sts with skin colour yarn and work an i-cord for 10 rows. Break yarn, draw through sts, pull tightly and fasten off.

Wings

Cast on 35 sts with white mohair yarn on 4mm (UK 8, US 6) needles.
Row 1: k.
Row 2: p2tog, p to last 2 sts, p2tog (33).
Repeat rows 1 and 2 until there are 25 sts left.
Decrease 1 st at both ends of every row until there are 17 sts left.
Cast off.

To make up

Sew the head and the body seam, leaving a gap for stuffing. Stuff, avoiding the neck area, and close the seam. Work a gathering thread around the neck and pull tightly. Work a gathering thread for the eye line (optional). Flatten the base of the body as shown on pages 17–18. Attach the arms to the sides of the body. Attach the legs to the front edge of the base of the body. Sew the seam of the skirt and attach the skirt to the waist, with the seam at the back. Using dark brown DK (8-ply) yarn, embroider a French knot for each eye. Create a nose by backstitching the same spot three times using skin colour DK (8-ply) yarn. To create the hair, take two strands from brown DK (8-ply) yarn and wrap them around four fingers twenty-five to thirty times – you can control the length of the hair as you wish. Attach the hair as shown on page 19, then trim the loop ends at the bottom.

Materials

DK (8-ply) yarn: 6g (1/5oz), light blue or pink

DK (8-ply) yarn: small amounts of skin colour, brown and dark brown

Fine mohair: small amount of white for the wings

Stuffing

Additional equipment

A pair of 4mm (UK 8, US 6) knitting needles

Size

8cm (3¼in) tall

Difficulty level

Beginner

To make up the wings, work a gathering thread from the centre of the cast-off edge of the wings to the centre of the cast-on edge of the wings, pull tightly and fasten. Hide the yarn ends inside the stitches and attach the wings to the back of the body.

Up-and-away!

Instructions

Balloon

Cast on 6 sts with white yarn.
Row 1: p.
Row 2: kf/b in each st (12).
Row 3: p.
Row 4: kf/b in each st (24).
Row 5: p.
Row 6: (k1, kf/b) to end (36).
Row 7: p.
Row 8: (k2, kf/b) to end (48).
Join in the six colours for the balloon, twisting the yarns at the back of the work when changing colour.
Row 9: p8 yellow, p8 light green, p8 light blue, p8 light purple, p8 red, p8 orange.
Row 10: keeping the colours correct, p for the edge.
Rows 11–25: keeping the colours correct, st/st, starting with a p row. Continue in st/st, keeping the colours correct whilst increasing and decreasing.
Row 26: (k2, kf/b, k2, kf/b, k2) to end (60).
Rows 27–33: st/st.
Row 34: (k2, k2tog) twice, (k4, k2tog, k2, k2tog) five times, k2 (48).
Row 35: p.
Row 36: (k2, k2tog) to end (36).
Row 37: p.
Row 38: (k1, k2tog) to end (24).
Row 39: p.
Row 40: (k2tog) to end (12).
Row 41: p.
Row 42: (k2tog) to end (6).
Break yarn, draw through sts, pull tightly and fasten off.

Basket

Using light brown yarn, follow the instructions given for the balloon until row 6.
Row 7: k for edge.
Rows 8–14: st/st, starting with a k row.
Rows 15–16: k.
Row 17: k for fold line.
Rows 18–19: st/st, starting with a k row.
Cast off.

To make up

Starting at the fasten-off end, sew the seam of the balloon halfway along. Work a gathering thread along the cast-on edge, pull tightly and fasten off. Stuff and close the seam.
To make up the basket, work a gathering thread along the cast-on edge and pull tightly. Sew the rest of the seam. Fold the piece at the folding line and secure the cast-off edge to the inner side of the basket.
Attach four strands of light brown yarn to the basket and connect the basket to the balloon. See the picture for guidance. Using white yarn, make a loop at the top of the balloon, to hang it up.

continued overleaf

Materials

Balloon and basket:

DK (8-ply) yarn: 4g ($\frac{1}{8}$oz), each of white, yellow, light green, light blue, light purple, red, orange and light brown

Stuffing

Boy:

DK (8-ply) yarn: small amounts of light green, light blue, white, skin colour, blue and dark brown

Stuffing

Dog:

DK (8-ply) yarn: small amounts of white and dark brown

Stuffing

Size

17cm (6¾in) from the top of the balloon to the bottom of the basket

Difficulty level

Beginner

Boy

Body and head

The body is knitted in striped st/st. Do not break the yarn each time you change colour. Slide the sts to the end of the needle and continue. Starting with the base, cast on 4 sts with light green yarn.

Row 1: p.
Row 2: kf/b in each st (8).
Row 3: p.
Row 4: (k1, kf/b) to end (12).
Row 5: k for edge.
Row 6: k.
Row 7: (p1, pf/b, p1) to end (16).
Row 8: change to light blue yarn and k.
Join in white yarn.
Row 9: p with white yarn, do not break yarn.
Row 10: k with light blue yarn. Slide the sts to the end of the needle and continue.
Row 11: k with white yarn. Break off white yarn.

Row 12: (p2, p2tog) to end with light blue yarn (12).
Break off light blue yarn.
Slide the sts to the end of the needle and continue.
Row 13: change to skin colour yarn and p.
Row 14: (k2, kf/b) to end (16).
Rows 15–19: st/st.
Row 20: (k2, k2tog) to end (12).
Break yarn, draw through sts, pull tightly and fasten off.

Arms: make two

Cast on 2 sts with skin colour yarn and work an i-cord for 3 rows. Break yarn, draw through sts, pull tightly and fasten off.

Cap

Cast on 17 sts with blue yarn.
Row 1: p.
Row 2: k.
Row 3: (p2, p2tog) to last st, p1 (13).

Row 4: (k2, k2tog) to last st, k1 (10).
Break yarn, draw through sts, pull tightly and fasten off.

Cap visor

With the right side facing and blue yarn, pick up 8 sts from the front edge of the cap.
Row 1: p.
Row 2: skpo, k to last 2 sts, k2tog (6). Cast off.

To make up

Follow the instructions given on pages 16–18 to make up the body and head and flatten the base. Attach the arms. Seam the cap and then attach it. Using dark brown DK (8-ply) yarn, embroider each eye with a French knot. Create a nose by backstitching on the same spot three times with skin colour yarn.

Dog

Body

Cast on 6 sts with white yarn.

Row 1: kf/b in each st (12).

Row 2: k for edge.

Rows 3–6: st/st, starting with a k row.

Row 7: (k1, k2tog, k1) to end (9).

Row 8: p.

Break yarn, draw through sts, pull tightly and fasten off.

Head

Cast on 12 sts with white yarn and st/st 4 rows, starting with p row.

Next row: (p1, p2tog) to end (8).

Break yarn, draw through sts, pull tightly and fasten off.

Ears: make two

Cast on 2 sts with white yarn, skpo and fasten off.

To make up

Sew the head seam, leaving a gap for stuffing. Stuff and close the seam. Sew the body seam, leaving a gap for stuffing. Stuff and close the seam. Attach the head to the body and the ears to the head. Using two strands taken from dark brown DK (8-ply) yarn, embroider each eye with a French knot and create a nose by backstitching on the same spot three times.

Prehistoric playtime

Instructions

Mammoth

Body, head, legs and trunk

Cast on 45 sts with dark brown yarn, starting with a k row.

Rows 1–14: st/st.

Row 15: cast off 6 sts, k to end (39).

Row 16: cast off 6 sts, p to end (33).

Row 17: cast on 3 sts, k to end (36).

Row 18: cast on 3 sts, p to end (39).

Rows 19–22: st/st.

Row 23: k10, kf/b, k17, kf/b, k to end (41).

Row 24: p.

Row 25: k11, kf/b, k8, kf/b, k8, kf/b, k to end (44).

Row 26: p.

Row 27: k12, kf/b, k9, kf/b, k8, kf/b, k to end (47).

Row 28: p.

Row 29: k13, kf/b, k9, kf/b, k9 kf/b, k to end (50).

Row 30: p.

Row 31: k14, kf/b, k10, kf/b, k9, kf/b, k to end (53).

Row 32: p.

Row 33: k15, kf/b, k21, kf/b, k to end (55).

Row 34: p.

Row 35: cast off 3, k to end (52).

Row 36: cast off 3, p to end (49).

Row 37: cast on 8, k these sts, k13, kf/b, k21, kf/b, k to end (59).

Row 38: cast on 8 sts, p to end (67).

Row 39: k20, kf/b, k25, kf/b, k to end (69).

Rows 40–48: st/st.

Row 49: cast off 8 sts, k to end (61).

Row 50: cast off 8 sts, p to end (53).

Row 51: cast off 8 sts, k to end (45).

Row 52: cast off 8 sts, p22, yb, sl1, yf, turn.

Row 53: sl1, k11, yf, sl1, yb, turn.

Row 54: sl1, p11, yb, sl1, yf, turn.

Row 55: sl1, k11, yf, sl1, yb, turn.

Row 56: sl1, p to end.

Row 57: k9, k2tog, k15, k2tog, k to end (35).

Row 58: p9, p2tog, p13, p2tog, p to end (33).

Row 59: k9, k2tog, k11, k2tog, k to end (31).

Row 60: p9, p2tog, p9, p2tog, p to end (29).

Row 61: k9, k2tog, k7, k2tog, k to end (27).

Rows 62–65: st/st.

Row 66: p, decreasing 1 st at each end of the row (25).

Rows 67–71: st/st.

Row 72: p, decreasing 1 st at each end of the row (23).

Rows 73–79: st/st.

Row 80: p, decreasing 1 st at each end of the row (21).

Rows 81–83: st/st.

Row 84: p, decreasing 1 st at each end of the row (19).

Work in st/st, decreasing 1 st at each end of every fourth row until 11 sts remain.

Next row: k2, k2tog, k3, k2tog, k2 (9).

Break yarn, draw through sts, pull tightly and fasten off.

Materials

Mammoth:

DK (8-ply) mohair yarn or DK (8-ply) yarn: 25g ($^9/_{10}$oz), dark brown

DK (8-ply) yarn: 7g (¼oz), white

DK (8-ply) yarn: small amount of black

Stuffing

Five cave people:

DK (8-ply) yarn: 8g (⅓oz), khaki

DK (8-ply) yarn: 10g (⅓oz), skin colour

Fine bouclé yarn: small amount of dark brown or two strands taken from DK (8-ply) yarn

DK (8-ply) yarn: small amounts of dark brown, brown and grey

Stuffing

Size

Mammoth: 15cm (5¾in) long, 11cm (4¼in) tall

Cave people: 4cm (1½in) tall

Difficulty level

Intermediate

Tusks: make two

Cast on 10 sts with white yarn.
Rows 1–23: st/st, starting with a p row.
Row 24: k, decreasing 1 st at each end of the row (8).
Rows 25–29: st/st.
Row 30: k, decreasing 1 st at each end of the row (6).
Rows 31–33: st/st.
Break yarn, draw through sts, pull tightly and fasten off.

Left ear

Cast on 8 sts with dark brown yarn.
Row 1: p.
Row 2: k to last 2 sts, k2tog (7).
Row 3: p2tog, p to end (6).
Cast off.

Right ear

Cast on 8 sts with dark brown yarn.
Row 1: p.
Row 2: skpo, k to end (7).
Row 3: p to last 2 sts, p2tog (6).
Cast off.

Tail

Cast on 3 sts with dark brown yarn and work an i-cord for 2cm (¾in).
Break yarn, draw through sts, pull tightly and fasten off.

To make up

Fold one hind leg in half vertically and work a gathering thread through the foot edge, pull tightly. Sew the rest of the leg seam. Sew the tummy flap to the cast-on edge. Pinch the rest of the cast-on edge together and sew together to create the bottom. Make up the second hind leg and the front legs as for the first hind leg. Starting at the fasten-off end, sew the trunk seam and attach the front of the tummy flaps to the trunk. Stuff the body, head, legs and trunk and close the tummy seam. Starting at the fasten-off end, sew the tusk seams, leaving a gap for stuffing. Stuff and close the seam. Attach the tusks. Attach the cast-off edge of each ear to the head. Using black DK (8-ply) yarn, embroider each eye with a French knot, and the trunk with backstitch. See the picture for guidance. Attach the tail.

Cave people

Body and head

Starting with the base, cast on 4 sts with khaki yarn.

Row 1: p.
Row 2: kf/b in each st (8).
Row 3: p.
Row 4: (k1, kf/b) to end (12).
Row 5: k for fold line.
Row 6: k.
Row 7: p.
Row 8: (k1, kf/b, k1) to end (16).
Rows 9–11: st/st.
Row 12: (k2, k2tog) to end (12).
Row 13: change to skin colour yarn and p.
Row 14: (k2, kf/b) to end (16).
Rows 15–19: st/st.
Row 20: (k2, k2tog) to end (12).
Break yarn, draw through sts, pull tightly and fasten off.

Arms: make two

Cast on 2 sts with skin colour yarn and work an i-cord for 3 rows.
Break yarn, draw through sts, pull tightly and fasten off.

Beard (optional)

Cast on 6 sts with dark brown fine bouclé yarn or two strands taken from dark brown DK (8-ply) yarn.

Row 1: k.
Row 2: skpo, k to end (5).
Row 3: skpo, k to end (4).
Row 4: (k2tog) twice (2).
Pass the first stitch over the second stitch and fasten off.

Rock for hammer top

Cast on 4 sts with grey yarn and st/st 4 rows, starting with a k row.
Break yarn, draw through sts, pull tightly and fasten off.

Hammer handle

Cast on 2 sts with brown yarn and work an i-cord for 3 rows.
Pass the first stitch over the second stitch and fasten off.

To make up

Follow the instructions on pages 16–18 to sew up the body and head and flatten the base. Attach the arms. Using dark brown DK (8-ply) yarn, embroider each eye with a French knot. Create a nose by backstitching on the same spot three times with skin colour yarn.

Attach the beard using dark brown bouclé yarn; alternatively, backstitch all over the chin until you achieve the desired volume.

With brown bouclé yarn, backstitch all over the head to create hair, until you reach the volume you want.

Fold the rock piece in half horizontally, enclosing one end of the handle, and secure the rock with a few stitches, using the brown yarn. Using the same yarn, embroider the middle of the rock, passing the yarn over to the other side, and repeat. Attach the hammer to a hand with skin colour yarn. Embroider the head of the hammer with two strands of brown DK (8-ply) yarn.

Castle under siege!

Instructions

Towers

Centre tower

Cast on 8 sts with grey yarn.
Row 1: p. .
Row 2: kf/b in each st (16).
Row 3: p.
Row 4: (k1, kf/b) to end (24).
Row 5: p.
Row 6: (k2, kf/b) to end (32).
Row 7: p.
Row 8: (k3, kf/b) to end (40).
Row 9: p.
Row 10: (k4, kf/b) to end (48).
Row 11: p.
Row 12: (k5, kf/b) to end (56).
Row 13: k for the edge.
Starting with a k row, st/st until the piece measures 9cm (3½in) from the edge. Finish with a p row.
* Change to dark red yarn and st/st 8 rows, starting with a k row.
Next row: (k2, k2tog) to end (42).
Work 4 rows in st/st, starting with a p row.
Next row: (p1, p2tog) to end (28).
Work 2 more rows in st/st.
Next row: (k2tog) to end (14).
Break yarn, draw through sts, pull tightly and fasten off. **

The left front tower

Follow the instructions given for the centre tower to row 8.
Row 9: k for the edge.
Starting with a k row, st/st until the piece measures 8cm (3¼in) from the edge. Finish with a p row.
Work from * to ** as given for the centre tower. The stitch count will be 30, 20, 10 sts respectively at the decrease rows.

The right front tower

Follow the instructions given for the centre tower to row 8.
Row 9: k for the edge.
Starting with a k row, st/st until the piece measures 8cm (3¼in) from the edge. Finish with a p row.
Continue as follows.
Row 1: (k3, k2tog) to end (32).
Row 2: p.
Row 3: (k2, k2tog) to end (24).
Row 4: p.
Row 5: (k1, k2tog) to end (16).
Row 6: p.
Row 7: (k2tog) to end (8).
Row 8: p.
Break yarn, draw through sts, pull tightly and fasten off.

Materials

Castle:

- DK (8-ply) yarn: 60g (2oz), grey

- DK (8-ply) yarn: 20g (¾oz), dark red

- DK (8-ply) yarn: 5g (⅙oz), brown

- DK (8-ply) yarn: small amount of white

Size

18cm (7in) tall, 16cm (6¼in) wide

Difficulty level

Intermediate

Rear towers: make two

Follow the instructions given for the centre tower to end of row 6.
Row 7: k for the edge.
Starting with a k row, st/st until the piece measures 13cm (5in) from the edge. Finish with a p row.
Work from * to ** as given for the centre tower. The stitch count will be 24, 16, 8 sts respectively at the decrease rows.

continued overleaf

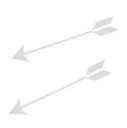

Battlements

The battlements for the towers start and finish with a short section, but do not worry. The seams go at the back of each tower, so they are hidden.

For the centre tower

Cast on 65 sts with grey yarn and st/st 5 rows, starting with a p row.
Next row: k5, turn and work on this set of 5 sts.
Next row: k for fold line.
St/st 4 rows starting with a k row, cast off these 5 sts.
* With the right side facing, rejoin grey yarn and knit the next 5 sts, turn. Work on this set of 5 sts.
St/st 4 rows, starting with a p row.
Next row: k for fold line.
St/st 6 rows, starting with a k row. Cast off these 5 sts.
** With the right side facing, rejoin grey yarn and knit the next 5 sts, turn. Work on this set of 5 sts.
Next row: k for fold line.
St/st 4 rows, starting with a k row. Cast off these 5 sts.
Continue in the same way, alternating working from * and from ** until all sts have been worked.
Sew the seams, folding at the fold lines.

For the front towers: make two

Cast on 40 sts with grey yarn and follow the instructions given for the centre tower battlements.

For the back towers: make two

Cast on 35 sts and follow the instructions given for the centre tower battlements.

Gate door

Cast on 15 sts with brown yarn.
Rows 1–14: st/st, starting with a k row.
Row 15: skpo, k to last 2 sts, k2tog (13).
Row 16: p.
Repeat rows 15 and 16 until there are 9 sts.
Cast off.

Windows: make two

Cast on 10 sts with white yarn.
Rows 1–5: st/st, starting with a p row.
Row 6: skpo, k to last 2 sts, k2tog (8).
Row 7: p.
Row 8: as row 6 (6).
Row 9: p2tog, cast off all the sts to the last 2 sts, p2tog and fasten off.

Making up

Starting at the fasten-off end of each tower, sew the seam, stopping where the colour changes. Work a gathering thread along the cast-on edge of each tower and pull tightly. Sew the rest of the base and side seam leaving a gap for stuffing. Stuff and close the seam. To flatten the base, insert a threaded needle through the centre of the base and bring it out at the side seam, about 4–5cm (1½–2in) from the base edge. Repeat. Attach a window to each front tower. Embroider the windowframes using brown DK (8-ply) yarn: create the outer frame using chain stitch, and the inside bars using long backstitches. Attach the gate door to the centre tower. Fold each battlement piece at the fold line and sew the seam. With the seam at the back and the cast-on edge at the bottom, attach a battlement around each tower where the colour changes, using overcast stitch. Sew the towers together, or leave them unattached so that children can enjoy building.

Soldier with chainmail

Body and head

Starting with the base, cast on 4 sts with light grey yarn.
Row 1: p.
Row 2: kf/b in each st (8).
Row 3: p.
Row 4: (k1, kf/b) to end (12).
Row 5: k for edge.
Row 6: k.
Row 7: (p1, pf/b, p1) to end (16).
Rows 8–11: st/st.
Row 12: (k2, k2tog) to end (12).
Change to skin colour yarn.
Row 13: p.
Row 14: (k2, kf/b) to end (16).
Rows 15–19: st/st.
Row 20: (k2, k2tog) to end (12).
Break yarn, draw through sts, pull tightly and fasten off.

Arms: make two

Cast on 2 sts with light grey yarn and work an i-cord for 3 rows (see page 21). Change to skin colour yarn and work one more row.
Break yarn, draw through sts, pull tightly and fasten off.

Chainmail

Cast on 20 sts with dark grey yarn.
Rows 1–3: st/st, starting with a
k row.
Row 4: p7, cast off next 6 sts, p to
end (14).
Row 5: k7, turn. Work on this set
of 7 sts.
Rows 6–9: st/st, starting with a
p row.
Break off yarn, leaving sts on
the needle.
With right side facing, rejoin dark
grey yarn to the other set of 7 sts.
Work on this set of 7 sts.
Rows 5–9: st/st, starting with a
k row.
Row 10: p across the row
connecting both sets of sts (14).
Row 11: (k2tog) to end (7).
Break yarn, draw through sts, pull
tightly and fasten off.

To make up

Follow the instruction given on
pages 16–18 to make up the
body and head and flatten the
base. Attach the arms. Sew the
chainmail seam and attach the
chainmail to the head, with the
seam at the back. Embroider each
eye with a French knot, using dark
brown DK (8-ply) yarn.
Create a nose by backstitching
on the same spot three times with
skin colour yarn.

Foot soldier with shield

Body and head

Cast on 4 sts with light grey yarn
and follow the instructions given
for the soldier with chainmail to
end of row 9. Work rows 10–12
with dark grey yarn and rows
13–20 with skin colour yarn.

Cap

Cast on 17 sts with dark grey yarn.
Row 1: (k1 dark grey, k3 brown) to
last st, k1 dark grey.
Row 2: keeping the colours
correct, p.
Row 3: keeping the colours correct,
(k2, k2tog) to last st, k1 (13).
Row 4: keeping the colours
correct, (p1, p2tog) to last st,
p1 (9).
Break yarn, draw through sts with
dark grey yarn, pull tightly and
fasten off.

Arms: make two

Follow the instructions given for
the soldier with chainmail, using
dark grey yarn for the sleeve and
skin colour for the hand.

Shield

Cast on 16 sts with light grey
DK (8-ply) yarn.
Row 1: p.
Row 2: (k2tog, k2) to end (12).
Row 3: (p2tog) to end (6).
Break yarn, draw through sts, pull
tightly and fasten off.

Beard

Cast on 6 sts with light brown fine
bouclé yarn.
Row 1: k.

Materials

Soldier with chainmail:

DK (8-ply) yarn: small amounts
of light grey, skin colour,
dark grey and dark brown

Stuffing

Foot soldier with shield:

DK (8-ply) yarn: small
amounts of light grey, dark
grey, skin colour, brown
and dark brown

Fine bouclé yarn: small
amount of light brown

Stuffing

Size

5cm (2in) tall

Difficulty level

Intermediate

Row 2: skpo, k to end (5).
Row 3: skpo, k to end (4).
Row 4: skpo, k to end (3).
Cast off.

To make up

Follow the instructions given on
pages 16–18 to make up the body
and head and flatten the base.
Starting at the fasten-off end, sew
the cap seam and attach the cap
to the head. Attach the arms and
the beard. Embroider each eye
with a French knot, using dark
brown DK (8-ply) yarn. Create a
nose by backstitching on the same
spot three times, with skin colour
yarn. Sew the shield seam and
attach the shield to one arm.

Soldier with armour, full face helmet

Body and head

Starting with the base, cast on 4 sts with off-white yarn. Follow the instructions given for the soldier with chainmail to row 12. Do not change colour, continue working with off-white yarn.

Row 13: p.
Row 14: (k1, kf/b) to end (18).
Rows 15–19: st/st.
Row 20: (k1, k2tog) to end (12).
Break yarn, draw through sts, pull tightly and fasten off.

Grey visor

Cast on 2 sts with grey yarn.
Row 1: kf/b, k1 (3).
Row 2: pf/b, p1, pf/b (5).
Row 3: kf/b, k to last st, kf/b (7).
Row 4: pf/b, p to last st, pf/b (9).
Row 5: skpo, k to last 2 sts, k2tog (7).
Row 6: p2tog, p to last 2 sts, p2tog (5).
Row 7: skpo, k1, k2tog (3).
Cast off.

Shield

Cast on 2 sts with white yarn.
Row 1: pf/b, p1 (3).
Row 2: kf/b, k1, kf/b (5).
Row 3: pf/b, p to last st, pf/b (7).
Join in red yarn.
Row 4: k3 white, k1 red, k3 white.
Row 5: keeping the colours correct, p.
Row 6: k2 white, k3 red, k2 white.
Row 7: p3 white, p1 red, p3 white.
Break off red and continue with white.
Row 8: k.

Row 9: p.
Row 10: p for fold line.
Row 11: p.
Rows 12–16: st/st, starting with a k row.
Row 17: p2tog, p3, p2tog (5).
Row 18: skpo, k1, k2tog (3).
Row 19: p1, p2tog (2).
Pass the first stitch over the second stitch and fasten off.

Shoulder pieces: make two

Cast on 8 sts with off-white yarn and st/st 2 rows, starting with a p row.
Break yarn, draw through sts, pull tightly and fasten off.

Arms: make two

Cast on 2 sts with grey yarn and work an i-cord for 4 rows (see page 21). Break yarn, draw through sts, pull tightly and fasten off.

To make up

Follow the instructions given on pages 16–18 to make up the body and head and flatten the base. Attach the visor to the face. Wrap a shoulder piece around the top of one arm and, starting at the fasten-off end of the shoulder seam, sew the seam. With the seam facing in towards the body, attach to the body. Repeat for the second arm and shoulder piece. With red DK (8-ply) yarn, backstitch a few times on the top of the head, leaving loops every other stitch. Cut the loops and separate the strands. Attach the shield to one of the arms.

Materials

Soldier with armour, full face helmet:

DK (8-ply) yarn: small amounts of off-white, grey, white and red

Stuffing

Soldier with armour, face showing:

DK (8-ply) yarn: small amounts of off-white, skin colour, grey, brown, dark brown and red

Stuffing

Size

5cm (2in) tall

Difficulty level

Intermediate

Soldier with armour, face showing

Body and head

Starting with the base, cast on 4 sts with off-white yarn. Follow the instructions given for the soldier with chainmail, using off-white yarn for the body and skin colour yarn for the head.

Helmet

Cast on 18 sts with off-white yarn.

Rows 1–4: st/st, starting with a p row.

Row 5: (p1, p2tog) to end (12).

Row 6: (k2tog) to end (6).

Break yarn, draw through sts, pull tightly and fasten off.

Helmet visors: make two

Cast on 9 sts with grey yarn.

Row 1: p.

Row 2: skpo, k to last 2 sts, k2tog (7).

Row 3: p2tog, p3, p2tog (5).

Row 4: skpo, k1, k2tog (3).

Row 5: sl1, p2tog (2).

Pass the first stitch over the second stitch and fasten off.

Arms, shoulder pieces: make two of each

As given for the soldier with armour, full face helmet.

Battle axe

Cast on 7 sts with grey yarn.

St/st, starting with a k row and decreasing 1 st at each end of every row until there are 3 sts.

Continue in st/st, increasing 1 st at each end of every row until there are 7 sts. Cast off.

For the handle, cast on 2 sts with brown yarn and work an i-cord for 6cm (2½in).

Pass the first stitch over the second stitch and fasten off.

Lance

Cast on 8 sts with grey yarn and st/st 4 rows, starting with a k row.

Row 5: k, decreasing 1 st at each end of the row (6).

Rows 6–8: st/st.

Row 9: (k2tog) to end (3).

Break yarn, draw through sts, pull tightly and fasten off.

For the handle, cast on 2 sts with grey yarn and work an i-cord for 6cm (2½in).

Pass the first stitch over the second stitch and fasten off.

To make up

Follow the instructions given on pages 16–18 to make up the body and head and flatten the base. Attach the helmet and visors. Embroider each eye with a French knot using dark brown DK (8-ply) yarn. With skin colour yarn, create the nose by backstitching on the same spot three times.

Wrap a shoulder piece around the top of one arm and, starting at the fasten-off end of the shoulder seam, sew the seam. With the seam facing in towards the body, attach to the body. Repeat for the second arm and shoulder piece. With red DK (8-ply) yarn, backstitch a few times on the top of the head, leaving loops every other stitch. Cut the loops and separate the strands.

To make up the battle axe, wrap the axe around one end of the handle and sew the cast-on and cast-off edges together. Secure to the handle with a few stitches using grey yarn.

To make up the lance, wrap the lance around one end of the handle and sew the seam. Secure to the handle with a few stitches using grey yarn.

Attach the lance or battle axe to an arm.

Archer

Body and head

Starting with the base, cast on 4 sts with blue yarn. Follow the instructions given for the soldier with chainmail to row 7.

Join in white yarn.

Row 8: k7 blue, k1 white, k8 blue.

Row 9: keeping the colours correct, p.

Row 10: k6 blue, k3 white, k7 blue.

Row 11: p8 blue, p1 white, p7 blue.

Row 12: keeping the colours correct, k2tog, k1, k2tog, k5, k2tog, k1, k2tog, k1 (12).

Change to skin colour yarn.

Row 13: p.

Row 14: (k2, kf/b) to end (16).

Rows 15–19: st/st.

Row 20: (k2, k2tog) to end (12).

Break yarn, draw through sts, pull tightly and fasten off.

Arms and shoulder pieces: make two of each

As given for the soldier with armour, full face helmet, using skin colour yarn for the arms and brown yarn for the shoulder pieces.

Helmet

Follow the instructions given for the soldier with armour, face showing, using grey yarn.

Bow

Cast on 2 sts with brown yarn and work an i-cord for 2cm (¾in), as explained on page 21.
Pass the first stitch over the second stitch and fasten off.

Beard (optional)

Follow the instructions given for the foot soldier, using fine red-brown bouclé yarn.

To make up

Follow the instructions given on pages 16–18 to make up the body and head and flatten the base. Wrap a shoulder piece around the top of one arm and, starting at the fasten-off end of the shoulder seam, sew the seam. With the seam facing in towards the body, attach to the body. Repeat for the second arm and shoulder piece. Seam and attach the helmet and attach the beard. Embroider each eye with a French knot using dark brown DK (8-ply) yarn (see page 22). To create the nose, backstitch on the same spot three times with skin colour yarn. Shape the bow, and attach a length of white fingering (4-ply) yarn to both ends. Attach the bow to one hand.

Prisoner

Body and head

Follow the instructions given for the soldier with chainmail, using black yarn for the body, white yarn for row 8 and row 10 and skin colour for the head.

Ball and chain

Cast on 8 sts with dark grey yarn.
Row 1: kf/b in each st (16).
Rows 2–6: st/st, starting with a p row.
Row 7: (k2tog) to end (8).
Break yarn, draw through sts, pull tightly and fasten off.
With white fingering (4-ply) yarn and a crochet hook, make a chain measuring 15cm (5¾in) long. Fasten off.

Arms: make two

Cast on 2 sts with skin colour yarn and work an i-cord for 4 rows. Break yarn, draw through sts, pull tightly and fasten off.

Hat

Cast on 18 sts with khaki yarn.
Rows 1–4: st/st, starting with a p row.
Row 5: (p1, p2tog) to end (12).
Rows 6–7: st/st.
Row 8: (k2tog) to end (6).
Break yarn, draw through sts, pull tightly and fasten off.

Beard

Follow the instructions given for the foot soldier, using dark brown fine bouclé yarn.

To make up

Follow the instruction given on pages 16–18 to make up the body and head and flatten the base. Attach the arms. Sew the hat seam and attach to the head. Attach the beard. Embroider each eye with a short backstitch using dark brown DK (8-ply) yarn. To create the nose, backstitch on the same spot three times with skin colour yarn.

To make up the ball, starting at the fasten-off end, sew the seam leaving a gap for stuffing. Stuff and close the seam. Attach the ball to the chain. Wrap the chain around the body and secure with a few small stitches.

Snow White and the seven dwarves

Instructions

Snow White

Body and head

Cast on 8 sts with yellow yarn.
Row 1: p.
Row 2: kf/b in each st (16).
Row 3: p.
Row 4: (k1, kf/b) to end (24).
Row 5: k for edge.
Rows 6–13: st/st, starting with a k row.
Row 14: (k2, k2tog) to end (18).
Change to blue yarn.
Rows 15–18: st/st.
Join in skin colour yarn.
Row 19: p7 blue, p4 skin colour, p7 blue.
Row 20: (k1 blue, k2tog blue) twice, k1 blue, (k1, k2tog, k1) skin colour, (k1, k2tog blue) twice, k1 blue (13).
Break off blue yarn and change to skin colour yarn.
Row 21: p.
Row 22: k4, (kf/b) five times, k4 (18).
Rows 23–25: st/st.
Row 26: k3, (k2tog, k1) four times, k3 (14).
Rows 27–29: st/st.
Row 30: k2 (k2tog, k2) to end (11).
Break yarn, draw through sts, pull tightly and fasten off.

Sleeves: make two

Cast on 8 sts with light blue yarn.
Row 1: (p1 red, p1 light blue) to end.
Break yarn, draw through sts, pull tightly and fasten off.

Arms: make two

Cast on 3 sts with skin colour yarn and work an i-cord for 4 rows.
Break yarn, draw through sts, pull tightly and fasten off.

To make up

See pages 16–19.

Materials

Snow White:

DK (8-ply) yarn: small amounts of yellow, blue, skin colour, light blue, red and dark brown

Fine fingering (2-ply) yarn: small amount of dark brown, or two strands taken from dark brown DK (8-ply) yarn

Stuffing

Size

8cm (3¼in) tall

Difficulty level

Intermediate

Dwarves: make seven in different colours

Materials

Seven dwarves:

DK (8-ply) yarn: small amounts of skin colour, dark brown and any colours of your choice

Bouclé yarn or chunky fleecy yarn: small amounts of colour of your choice for the beard

Stuffing

Size

4cm (1½in) tall

Difficulty level

Intermediate

Body and head

Starting with the base, cast on 4 sts with yarn in the colour of your choice, for the body.

Row 1: p.
Row 2: kf/b in each st (8).
Row 3: p.
Row 4: (k1, kf/b) to end (12).
Row 5: k for the edge.
Row 6: k.
Row 7: (p1, pf/b, p1) to end (16).
Rows 8–11: st/st.
Row 12: (k2, k2tog) to end (12).
Change to skin colour yarn.
Row 13: p.
Row 14: (k2, kf/b) to end (16).
Rows 15–19: st/st.
Row 20: (k2, k2tog) to end (12).
Break yarn, draw through sts, pull tightly and fasten off.

Beard

Cast on 6 sts with bouclé yarn or chunky fleecy yarn in the colour of your choice.

Rows 1–2: k.
Row 3: skpo, k2, k2tog (4).
Row 4: (k2tog) twice (2).
Pass the first stitch over the second stitch and fasten off.

Hat

Cast on 16 sts with yarn in the colour of your choice.

Rows 1–8: st/st, starting with a k row.
Row 9: k1, (k2tog, k1) to end (11).
Row 10: p.
Break yarn, draw through sts, pull tightly and fasten off.

To make up

Follow the instructions given on pages 16–18 to make up the body and head and flatten the base. Sew the hat seam and attach it to the head. Attach the beard.

To create the nose, backstitch on the same spot three times with skin colour yarn. Embroider each eye with a French knot, using dark brown DK (8-ply) yarn.

Materials
Cottage:

DK (8-ply) yarn:
   20g (¾oz), light brown

DK (8-ply) yarn: 10g (⅓oz)
   brown and white mix

DK (8-ply) yarn: small amounts
   of brown and white

DK (8-ply) yarn: small
   amounts of red, pink,
   yellow and green for
   embroidering flowers

Chunky yarn: 10g (⅓oz),
   red or red DK (8-ply) yarn
   knitted double

Stuffing

Additional equipment
A pair of 4mm (UK 8, US 6)
knitting needles

Size
11cm (4¼in) wide, 5cm (2in)
deep, 15cm (5¾in) high

Difficulty level
Intermediate

Cottage

Front and back panels: make one of each

Cast on 28 sts with light brown yarn and k 4 rows.

St/st, starting with k row for 5cm (2in), ending with a p row.

Next row: k1, skpo, k to last 3 sts, k2tog, k1 (26).

Next row: p.

Repeat last 2 rows until 4 sts remain.

Next row: skpo, k2tog (2).

Pass the first st over the second st and fasten off.

Side panels: make two

Cast on 14 sts with light brown yarn and k 4 rows.

St/st, starting with a k row for 5cm (2in), ending with a p row. Cast off.

Decoration

Cast on 6 sts with brown and white mix yarn.

Rows 1–3: st/st, starting with a k row.

Row 4: k.

Repeat rows 1–4 until the piece measures about 30cm (11¾in). Cast off.

Door

Cast on 10 sts with brown yarn.

Rows 1–10: st/st, starting with a k row.

Row 11: skpo, k to last 2 sts, k2tog (8).

Row 12: p.

Rows 13–16: repeat rows 11–12 twice more (4).

Row 17: k1, k2tog, k1 (3).

Cast off.

Base

Cast on 28 sts with light brown yarn and st/st 21 rows, starting with a k row. Cast off.

Windows: make three

Cast on 10 sts with white yarn and st/st 9 rows, starting with a k row. Cast off.

Roof

Cast on 12 sts with chunky red yarn or red DK (8-ply) yarn knitted double and 4mm (UK 8, US 6) knitting needles. Work in g-st for 19cm (7½in). Cast off.

To make up

Attach one window and the door to the front panel. Attach two windows to the back panel. Embroider the windows as shown in the diagram, using DK (8-ply) yarn in different colours. Embroider a door knob using green DK (8-ply) yarn. Sew the front, back and side panels together and stuff. Attach the base and the roof. Attach the decoration and embroider, using the diagrams of the window and flowers given below as guidance.

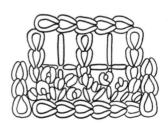